LIFE IN THE LEFT LANE

Emy Thomas

ISBN: 1-4033-0012-7

This book is printed on acid free paper.

1stBooks - rev. 02/25/02

Also by Emy Thomas

Non-Fiction

Home Is Where the Boat Is

Acknowledgements

The author wishes to thank Connie Underhill, patient and supportive friend and editor throughout the writing and numerous rewritings of this book;

Nina York, Wayne James, Sondra Catts, Liz Wilson and Tom Thomas for thoughtful readings and valuable comments;

Members of The Writers' Circle of St. Croix (Roz Hughes, Priscilla Watkins, Emeline Sprankle, Lolita Paiewonsky, Pat Murphy, Sharon Reynolds, Marge Tonks, Marty Campbell, Dennis McCluster, Art Merrill, Dick Matthews, Al Rymsha and the late Betty Dale) for their attention to details, chapter by chapter. Also the V.I. Family Sports & Fitness Center for generously providing its conference room for The Writers' Circle's weekly workshops;

And the many people who responded to my requests for information or help, including Bradley Christian, Deirdre Cooper, Trilby Shuie, Bob Carpenter, Janet Connally, Cindy Auth, Jayne Edwards, Liz Wilson, Barry Allaire, Onaje Jackson, Marjorie Robbins, Edwin Cordero and Tom Robinson.

Dedication

To my brother,
Philip H. Thomas Jr.
"Tom"

Table of Contents

Expatriates in Paradise

Every alluring tropical island has among its inhabitants a small subculture of expatriates from the "real world" who came by choice, survived the culture shock and have adopted it as their home.

They balance the simple pleasures of an idyllic lifestyle with the complex surprises of a foreign culture in an ongoing adventure that is never predictable and usually quite a lot of fun.

I am one of them, a transplant from the cold and crowded northeastern U. S. to the warm and wondrous Caribbean.

My personal paradise is St. Croix in the Virgin Islands, a realm celebrated for dazzling white beaches and clear turquoise waters, too beautiful to believe. A cluster of a hundred small islands and cays in the northeastern Caribbean, the Virgins are roughly one-third British, two-thirds "American Paradise."

St. Croix (pronounced Croy), the largest of the U.S. Virgin Islands, is a well-kept secret. Separated by 40 miles of ocean from the rest of the Virgins, it is nothing like its better-known siblings, St. Thomas the Lively Virgin, the most popular cruise ship port in the Caribbean, and St. John the Pure, a magnificent natural haven that is mostly National Park.

1

St. Croix is the Gentle Virgin. Its beauty is serene, its manner mild, and its people (Crucians or Cruzans) are, like the climate, mostly sunny and warm.

In this mellow setting the pace is slow, the atmosphere is informal and relaxed, and the prevailing attitude is carefree. "No problem" is a favorite expression.

Among the outsiders living here are a few thousand from the mainland U.S.A. We call ourselves continentals, mainlanders or statesiders. Since most of us are white, Crucians, who are mostly black, call us simply white people. As Americans in an American territory we are not technically expatriates, though we are often as bewildered as they are.

Statesiders who choose the U.S.V.I. precisely because it is American are in for a surprise. It can be quite traumatic to discover that, despite the flag, the islands are fundamentally Caribbean in style and the territory is more like a foreign country than another state.

For settlers accustomed to stateside efficiency and life in the fast lane, island style is full of puzzling paradoxes and frustrating foibles. Very few things start on time, hardly anyone plans ahead, logic is elusive, and simple errands routinely morph into monumental missions.

The phenomenon is called Crucian confusion or, in a phrase that has become a metaphor for quirky island style, life in the left lane. Yes, here in the U.S.V.I. we drive on the left-hand side of the road in cars designed to travel on the right.

Outsiders who embrace the style and enjoy life in the left lane are a special breed: adventurous, adaptable and accepting, with a good sense of the ridiculous.

2

An often-invoked calypso title that aptly describes the island outlook is "Don't Worry, Be Happy." I can't think of a better mantra to live by.

Discovering the Tropics

The first time I went to a tropical island, in 1962, I stepped off the plane in San Juan, Puerto Rico, felt the soft breeze caress me and thought I had arrived in heaven.

I was 28, a newspaper reporter on a one-week vacation from freezing New York. I wasn't looking for a new life, just a few days playing in the sun and maybe a Latin romance. My seduction by the island itself took me by surprise. I loved everything about the tropical ambience, especially the climate—hot but not humid, thanks to that ever-present tradewind and its gentle touch.

I was also delighted by the music, bouncy and happy, and the loose, joyful way people broke out dancing whenever, wherever, they heard it. I was thrilled by the jungly vegetation—the exotic colors and shapes of the flowers, the grace of feathery palms, the drama of giant-size bushes and trees. I was captivated by the sultry scent of night-blooming jasmine. And I adored the voluptuous flavors of tropical fruits—the slurpy mango and the puckery lime. My senses had never been so charged, or charmed.

One day I flew in a tiny plane to nearby St. Croix to see a friend from my hometown in Connecticut who had settled there. I was amazed to find I liked this quiet, sparsely-developed little island even more than Puerto Rico and that

I related to the lifestyle of my once-preppie friend, an architect, who was working in cut-off shorts and bare feet.

I had never been anywhere with so much natural beauty and I couldn't get over the awesome views around every corner. The colors of the water especially blew me away— turquoise and jade, sapphire and emerald, like gems.

I was delighted by every glimpse I had of island life: smiling people, comfortable clothes, the slow pace, the casual mixing of races, the fading grandeur of public buildings, the informality of shops and restaurants.

I had never questioned what I was doing with my life but suddenly I realized I could do much better. This could be my scene. I too could be relaxed and happy in a beautiful, delightful environment, and I never had to be cold again.

It could have been a passing fantasy but a few years later, when three New York newspapers folded after a long strike and I lost my dream job on the *Herald Tribune*, I boarded that plane to paradise again and I've been in the islands ever since.

I didn't go to St. Croix immediately, guessing that I couldn't make a living there. First I found newspaper work in San Juan. Then I lucked into a fabulous tropical odyssey when I fell in love with a "yachtie," Peter Hansen, who was sailing around the world. I went along with him for 13 years, cruising slowly throughout the Caribbean and Pacific, island-hopping wherever the tradewinds blew us.

We visited scores of islands, some legendary, some rarely seen. I liked almost every one of them and could picture myself living on a few, but St. Croix continued to beckon. I can't explain rationally the lure of this particular island. It just felt right for me.

By the time we reached the South China Sea, where piracy was a fact of life, I was so frightened I decided it was time to quit the cruising scene. Peter was understanding. We planned that I would go to St. Croix and build my dream house while he completed his circumnavigation, then we would reunite in St. Croix.

Those plans changed and he never sailed back into my life, but I have never regretted my decision to abandon ship nor my choice of location. My intuition was right. St. Croix is "home."

The Lure of the Caribbean

The enticing islands of the Caribbean have always attracted adventurers seeking a desirable place to live.

For hundreds of years before the white man or the black man, indigenous tribes moved through the region, living well off the land and sea. Throughout the islands they left scattered evidence of their villages, their ceremonial sites and burial grounds.

The glorious archipelago that borders the Caribbean Sea includes The Greater Antilles (the larger islands like Puerto Rico, Hispaniola and Cuba on the northern rim) and The Lesser Antilles (a chain of many small islands on the eastern rim). Like a crescent of stepping stones, the chain starts with the Virgin Islands in the north and continues through the Windward and Leeward Islands to South America.

Most of the islands have spectacular green mountains in the interior and inviting turquoise bays scalloping the shoreline, fringed with sandy beaches and palm trees swaying in the wind.

Christopher Columbus discovered these picture-postcard islands during two voyages in 1492 and 1493. He named them the West Indies when he realized he hadn't reached the East Indies after all.

Europeans were immediately eager to colonize the area. The islands were strategically important as the gateway to the Spanish Main, its gold and other treasures, and, thanks to fertile volcanic soil and the summery climate year-round, they had tremendous agricultural potential.

As the Spanish, French, English and Dutch fought each other for control, some of the islands changed hands many times and frequently more than one country occupied one small island at a time. Substantial forts still stand on many shores, reminders of that embattled period.

Pirates or buccaneers and privateers were also drawn to the West Indies. They used the islands' sheltered coves and bays as hideouts between attacks on treasure-laden ships sailing from South America to Europe.

While the Europeans clashed dramatically with each other, they casually annihilated the native "Indians." Very few aborigines survived the colonists' genocide, enslavement or diseases. Today the only living descendants of pre-Columbian people in the Caribbean are small communities of Caribs on Dominica and St. Vincent and some mixed-heritage inhabitants of The Greater Antilles.

Another horrifying fact of the colonial era was, of course, the importation of slaves from Africa. Between the 16th and 19th centuries, when plantations flourished throughout the region, the planters acquired their vast labor forces through the barbaric triangular trade. Ships sailing between Europe, West Africa and the Caribbean transported enslaved human beings as the "cargo" on the middle passage. Most of them spent the rest of their lives at hard labor in the sugarcane fields.

After the Africans finally won their freedom in the 1800s (emancipation on most of the islands pre-dated that in the U.S.), the balance of power slowly started to flip-flop. Today their descendants are by far the largest population group in the Eastern Caribbean. They have gradually assumed leadership on most of the islands, generally peacefully.

Although Martinique and Guadeloupe are still *departments* of France, the islands that were formerly British, Dutch and Spanish now have governments that are more or less autonomous. Several are totally independent: Cuba, Jamaica, Haiti, the Dominican Republic, Antigua/Barbuda, St. Christopher (St. Kitts)/ Nevis, Dominica, St. Lucia, Barbados, St. Vincent and the Grenadines and Grenada.

The U.S. became a player late in the game, acquiring Puerto Rico after the Spanish-American War and buying the Danish West Indies during World War I, to keep German commerce and military action out of the Caribbean and the Panama Canal. The price for the islands now known as the U.S.V.I. was $25 million.

The Gentle Virgin

Unlike most of the Caribbean islands, which are volcanic and dramatic, St. Croix has a gentle beauty. Rounded mountains give way to rolling hills that sweep down to lovely beaches and bays over more flat, fertile land than any other island in the Eastern Caribbean. Columbus found it extensively cultivated by Amerindians, and during the centuries of colonial rule St. Croix was famous as "the garden spot of the Caribbean."

Although crop agriculture is no longer significant, the island still has a tranquil, pastoral feel, with cattle grazing on miles of wide open land and fields of tall grass rippling like waves.

Only 84 miles square (28 east to west by 7 north to south at its widest point), it is by Virgin Islands standards The Big Island. Shaped like a slipper, the island goes to topographical extremes with almost-desert landscapes in the eastern toe and a not-quite rainforest in the western heel.

St. Croix's rare fertility made it highly popular throughout history. The aboriginal tribes that settled here have been identified as the Igneri (AD50-650), Taino or Arawak (AD 650-1425) and Kalina or Carib (AD 1425-1590). AyAy and Cibuguiera were Indian names for the island.

Salt River Bay, an area rich in natural resources, was the site of their principal settlement. Archeological finds there include petroglyphs from a Taino ceremonial ball park, the only one ever discovered in the Lesser Antilles, and a burial ground pre-dating Columbus by 1000 years.

Not surprisingly, this bay also attracted Christopher Columbus as he sailed along the north shore of St. Croix during his second voyage of discovery. He anchored his fleet of 17 caravels off the bay on November 14, 1493. Although the explorer himself didn't set foot ashore, members of his crew did, making Salt River the site of both the expedition's only documented landing on what is now U.S. soil and its first recorded hostile encounter with inhabitants of the New World.

According to ships' logs, a longboat with a crew of 25 men went ashore to a Carib village on the west bank looking for fresh water. The villagers fled, leaving behind several Arawak slaves, who were promptly appropriated by the sailors.

On its way back to the ships, the longboat encountered a Carib canoe emerging from the eastern headland and rammed it. The Caribs retaliated with bows and arrows until overpowered by the Europeans, who then captured the entire crew as slaves—four men, two women and a boy. Each side in this altercation had one fatality.

Columbus named the eastern point *Cabo de las Flechas* (Cape of the Arrows) to commemorate the confrontation. He named the island *Santa Cruz* (Holy Cross). As he sailed north into the cluster of many lovely small islands he reportedly thought of the legend of St. Ursula and her

11,000 virgins and christened the group *Islas de las Virgenes*.

Santa Cruz was translated as Sainte Croix by the French colonists that followed, and later the pronunciation was anglicized to Croy. The site of the Indian village is now a popular beach known as Columbus Landing.

After Columbus' "discovery," when Europeans fought for holdings in the Caribbean, St. Croix changed hands frequently. It is distinguished by the seven flags that flew here. They are: Spanish (1493-1641), British (1641-43 and 1645-50), Dutch (1643-45), French and the French-owned Knights of Malta (1650-1695), Danish (1733-1917) and the U.S.A. (1917-Present). The last two exchanges were peaceful. Denmark purchased the island from France and almost 200 years later sold it and the other Danish West Indies to the U.S.

The long Danish rule had a lasting influence on the island. Its two lovely towns, stately Christiansted in the east and quaint Frederiksted in the west, were both originally built in the imposing Danish Colonial style, with shaded arcades to protect pedestrians from the tropical sun. After Frederiksted was burned in a post-slavery labor uprising, in 1878, it was rebuilt in the then-current Victorian style. (In 2001, both towns are slowly being restored after years of deterioration from hurricanes and neglect.)

Out in the countryside, where the Danes divided the land into 375 plantations of about 150 acres each, the landscape is still punctuated with the remains of 118 sugar mills, conical windmills in which sugarcane was pressed when the island was a leading producer of sugar and its byproducts, molasses and rum.

Some are in excellent condition. There are also several elegant greathouses from that period, restored as public attractions or private homes. Building materials included local stone, bricks brought across the Atlantic as ballast, and coral from the sea. Molasses was used as an ingredient in mortar.

Areas of the island are still called by their evocative estate names such as Judith's Fancy, Jolly Hill, Hard Labour, Prosperity and Golden Grove.

Since few Danes were interested in being planters, the government opened the island to other settlers, mostly English, Irish and Scots who had owned or managed plantations on other Caribbean islands. Thus English became the common language. Crops included cotton, indigo and tobacco, but sugarcane was by far the most lucrative.

When development of the sugar beet replaced the need for sugarcane, St. Croix and other islands were forgotten by the outside world. They were discovered once again when the advent of air travel made them readily accessible and new generations learned about the joys of a tropical island escape.

Today, like most islands in the Eastern Caribbean, St. Croix depends on tourism for revenue. Unlike most of the other islands, we also have heavy industry. In the 1960s, Hess Oil built the largest oil refinery in the Western Hemisphere on the south shore of this American paradise. Next to it is an alumina refinery that has been operated on and off by a succession of companies. Smokestacks are a big surprise in a tropical paradise, but St. Croix is capacious enough to absorb the intrusion with ease.

The White Minority

On almost all the islands in the Eastern Caribbean the dominant population group is black West Indian, and white residents are a small minority. That is certainly true on St. Croix, which has only about 5,000 Caucasians, less than 10 percent of the permanent population. There is a smattering of old white planter families dating from the colonial era, but most are more recent arrivals, statesiders who have willingly relinquished their majority status for the pleasure of living in paradise.

St. Croix has an unusually diverse society, even for this part of the world. Native Crucians are almost outnumbered by "down-islanders," West Indians from other islands who have migrated here. Together they make up about 60 percent of the 53,000 population. Although they are not indigenous to the Caribbean, or West Indies, the descendants of Africans are called West Indians in the absence of any aboriginal natives.

A surprisingly large Puerto Rican population, at least 35 percent, is traced mostly to the island of Vieques. One wave of immigrants came in the 1920s to work in the cane fields. Another followed in the 1950s, after the U.S. Navy bought three-quarters of their island for bombing practice. Now there are more Viequenses on Santa Cruz than on their own island.

The island has also welcomed other Hispanics, African-Americans, Asians, East Indians, Europeans and Arabs, all seeking employment or the good life in a U.S. territory. Arabs, mostly from Palestine, account for about six percent of the population.

I like to think that most of the white mainlanders who have moved here voluntarily enjoy the racial diversity of the island. I know there are some who don't feel "safe" except in private clubs and neighborhoods like the East End, known as "the white ghetto." But for the rest of us, the desire for more cosmopolitan neighbors and friends was probably among the reasons we decided to leave home.

One of the best features of living here is the open society, where most people don't care much about where you're from, what you do, what you're worth or any other pigeonhole. Rich or poor, old or young, gay or straight, black or white, most people feel welcome and find it easy to make friends. This is the only place I've ever lived where I feel a part of the community. Even the few celebrities who have homes here are able to blend in.

West Indians have a refreshingly indifferent attitude toward monetary worth. And except for a small radical fringe that openly resents the white presence in this former slave colony, most of them are too polite to show any ill will they might feel toward any minority.

Here as on most of the Eastern Caribbean islands, small-town neighborliness and old-fashioned courtesy are still the norm, at least among the older people. They greet each other with good morning, good afternoon or good night (instead of good evening for some reason), and take the time to exchange pleasantries.

West Indians can be reserved with strangers, sometimes to the point of apparent rudeness, but if we initiate a polite greeting, we usually receive a similar response. Outgoing outsiders who demonstrate genuine friendliness are almost always rewarded with an amiable smile.

When I sense negative vibes it's usually because I've lapsed into New Yorker mode—I'm hurrying, avoiding eye contact, oblivious to the people passing by, forgetting to say good day. I'm not in the left lane, and it's my behavior, not my skin color, that has offended.

Snowbirds

"Snowbirds" are a species of humans who are winter residents of the islands. Like their feathered counterparts, they migrate every year to escape the cold of the north and bask in our perpetual summer. Most snowbirds are white. Some of them are indistinguishable from tourists, others are deeply involved with the island scene. Many snowbirds own a house or condominium here but home, their main nest, is still back in "civilization." A few snowbirds make the island their official residence for financial purposes; if they come from a state with an income tax, they can save substantially by filing here.

Another Beautiful Day

A perfect climate is a principal reason many of us choose to live in the islands. Coming from regions where almost every day is either too hot or too cold, we revel in the predictable succession of one beautiful day after another.

Let me quickly add (before everyone rushes down and spoils the place) that my definition of perfect isn't universally accepted. The islands are not far above the equator, spanning the latitudes from 10 to 20. Many people find the tropical temperatures simply too damn hot!

In St. Croix, which is at Latitude 17.7N and Longitude 64.8W, it is in the 80s every day. In the winter it is in the low 80s, dipping into the 70s at night, and in the summer it is in the high 80s, creeping into the 90s at midday. Those few degrees are all that differentiate our "seasons".

December through March are the coolest months. Those of us who have been in the tropics long enough to have "thin blood" actually feel the "winter." We sleep under light blankets, we wear sweaters or jackets in the evening and we don't go swimming for the duration.

The tradewinds that blow in the tropical latitudes are largely responsible for the pleasant climate. They can range from a gentle breeze to gusty, blustery 20- and 30-knot blows known locally as "Christmas winds."

My house is about 200 feet above sea level, facing the easterly winds. At that height the air is in almost constant motion. I keep my doors and windows wide open and let the breezes blow through. I seldom use my ceiling fans and have absolutely no need for air conditioning.

Rain rarely affects our daily routine in the Virgin Islands. Once in a great while we have a rainy day, but usually our precipitation is in the form of brief, localized showers or squalls that pass in minutes. The downfall can be heavy but soon the sun comes out and once again it's another beautiful day.

Most days the atmosphere is clear, with cerulean blue sky and puffy white cotton-ball clouds, gorgeous sunrises and sunsets, and awesome night skies brimming with stars and an exceptionally bright moon.

From my house on the north shore it is frequently clear enough to see St. Thomas and St. John 40 miles away and often the British Virgin Islands farther to the northeast. On the west end of St. Croix the mountains of Puerto Rico, 70 miles away, now and then come into view.

A thrilling atmospheric phenomenon on clear evenings is The Green Flash, a sunset event when conditions are just right. Though sometimes spectacular, it is often barely perceptible, and skeptics consider it a vision dependent on alcohol or a myth manufactured by beachfront bar owners to lure customers at sundown. I'm a believer because I've frequently seen it. When the ocean is flat and the western sky absolutely clear, just as the topmost curve of the setting sun drops below the horizon line, there is a momentary gleam of green.

There are days when the atmosphere can turn quite hazy, usually in the summer because of Sahara dust. It's hard to comprehend but it's a fact that sand from the Sahara Desert in Africa is picked up by the tradewinds and carried across the Atlantic Ocean to arrive in the Caribbean as a fine red dust. The dust is a housekeeping annoyance, of course, but more importantly it can aggravate respiratory conditions and scientists now think it may be contributing to the degradation of coral reefs.

Another source of dust closer to home is the Soufriere Volcano in Montserrat, 135 miles to the southeast. Whenever it erupts, our atmosphere goes into mourning for a day or so, and a gritty gray fallout is a sad reminder of our neighbors whose "emerald isle" is now covered in ash.

All That Energy

With such an abundance of sunshine and wind, the tropics is an ideal place to produce alternative sources of energy but, sadly, as I write in 2001, there is little use of renewable resources in the V.I. Few consumers are foresighted (or solvent) enough to invest in expensive windmills and solar panels, even though the equipment could pay for itself within a few years. And, although the federal energy office offers rebates on low-energy appliances, the territorial power authority has not yet risen to the challenge of working with consumers who make their own electricity.

Only a handful of projects, mostly private homes, are "off the grid". One with international recognition is Maho Bay Camps, Inc., a complex of eco-resorts in St. John created by Stanley Selengut, a pioneer in sustainable eco-tourism. There everything runs on solar-powered electricity, even an oven that bakes bread. In addition, bungalows are a showcase of recycled materials—tiles made of glass, decking made from newspapers, and siding that looks like wood planking made of cement and cardboard. I'd love to see industry on St. Croix that turns our trash into products like these.

On Island Time

The tem-po is slo-o-ow in the islands. West Indians move at a lei-sure-ly, graceful pace, with economy of motion, like a ballet. Many statesiders interpret the minimal activity as laziness but really, why work up a sweat? It's common sense to let the climate set the pace. Take it easy, mon, relax.

Continentals fresh from the rat-race go into culture shock when they find the laid-back island ambience extends to such concepts as appointments, schedules and deadlines. Only a few things, like church, start at the designated hour. In St. Croix we call the phenomenon Crucian time.

Those on Crucian time do not worship the clock. They apparently consider a given starting time a target to reach as soon as it's convenient. Whether getting to work or attending a meeting or social event, they arrive if and when they can. Although the attitude is enviably stressless, the practice can be maddening to those still hung up on puritan "virtues" like punctuality and reliability.

Most West Indians function on island time and accept it as the norm. Their patience as they wait for latecomers or stand in line or cool their heels at a bus stop seems limitless.

The most popular events, like reggae concerts and carnival parades, exploit that tolerance most flagrantly. Concerts planned for 8 o'clock have been known to start at midnight, with the headliner finally appearing a couple of hours later. Parades set to start at 10 or 11 in the morning actually set off sometime in the afternoon.

In the Spanish Caribbean, island time combines with the Latin propensity to put things off until *mañana* and outsiders don't have a clue what to expect. When I lived in Puerto Rico I soon found out that getting to a dinner party on time is a social *faux pas*. The hostess was still in the shower, she hadn't set the table yet and none of the other guests arrived for at least another hour.

A perplexing extension of island time is not showing up at all. This is quite common behavior, and it's accepted quite casually by other West Indians. One who tried to explain the practice to me called it a form of natural courtesy. Because it's not kind to say No, he always says Yes, whether he means it or not. Out of a desire to please the other person, to not disappoint, he makes appointments he has no intention of keeping.

What about the other person's disappointment later, when he realizes he's been stood up? My friend couldn't foresee a problem. He lives for the moment and expects others to do the same.

Worrying about the future and planning ahead are not compatible with island time. Even some business people are so unconcerned about tomorrow, stock for the store or supplies for the office aren't reordered until they run out.

Doing without is part of island adjustment. You know you're getting there when shortages, like punctuality, grow less and less important. Eventually you might even believe it's No Problem.

Emy Thomas

Making a Living

The cost of living is high in the islands, and making a living is a challenge, but many statesiders eagerly work at humble jobs and willingly make economic sacrifices for the privilege of being in paradise.

When I moved to Puerto Rico I continued to work in my profession—journalism—but I made half the salary I had in New York. I adapted. By the time I came to St. Croix I had burned out on journalism and I wasn't interested in trying a new career, but I did need to make some money.

Typical of the continentals here, I juggled a few income-producing enterprises. Jobs are not plentiful in St. Croix, especially in the off-season. Anyone who needs to make a living but does not have a profession or business is sometimes forced to be quite creative, patching together a crazy schedule of multiple part-time jobs and turning hobbies, like crocheting or making jams, into money-making projects.

At one point I worked in a small business office weekday mornings and in a gift shop on Saturdays and some afternoons. At the same time I tried my hand at selling catalog products to friends and acquaintances, I rented out my guest room and wrote a few free-lance articles.

It is refreshingly unimportant to have a prestigious occupation here, at least among the statesider population, many of whom "dropped out" because of stressful careers. Although I was certainly not living up to my potential, I never felt demeaned by the work I did. It was all part of island style.

Sometimes a new career is a primary purpose of relocating. A classic scenario has a stressed-out corporate type escaping to the islands to kick back under the palm trees and dabble in a simple business—say a small hotel. It's the *Don't Stop the Carnival* syndrome, after Herman Wouk's novel on that theme.

The irony is that trying to do business in the islands can be so confusing, frustrating and infuriating that the escapee simply swaps one set of stresses for another. Life in the left lane has defeated many a would-be entrepreneur, but there are many others who adjust, adapt and accommodate to make it work. If they're principals in a company that qualifies for EDA (Economic Development Authority) benefits, tax savings often sweeten the difficulties.

St. Croix quietly became a communications crossroads in the 1990s with the construction of two fiber optic cable facilities. With EDA incentives, the island is positioned to become a center of light high-tech industry—a bright prospect on the horizon for the economy and for making a living.

Expenses are surprisingly high in the islands. True, we don't have to heat our homes or buy winter clothes. Property taxes are lower than most places in the states but, because of hurricanes, homeowner's insurance with windstorm coverage is high. And, contrary to a common fantasy about paradise, one cannot live off the land and sea.

Certainly not in the Virgin Islands, where there is little agriculture and coastal waters are over-fished. Most of our food is flown or shipped in from the states or other islands and has a hefty mark-up. The little we have of locally-grown produce is equally high. It's hard to believe but a local mango can cost up to $3, even at a roadside stand. That's the same fruit you can buy in a stateside supermarket for under a dollar.

Other consumer goods, especially big-ticket items like electronic equipment and cars, are so high-priced we do our shopping when we're in the states or turn to catalogs and the Internet. I'm sure that most of us would prefer to support the local economy, which surely needs all the help it can get, but when there's a difference of thousands of dollars it's hard to justify that option. Even so, local businesses manage to survive because there are apparently enough people who don't have the time, interest or ability to look elsewhere.

The biggest expense here as everywhere is shelter— buying or renting a place to live. Real estate prices in St. Croix have fluctuated madly since I've been here. I bought my land and built my house when prices were reasonable. Within months St. Croix was suddenly "in" again (I like to take credit for being a trend-setter) and prices soared. They came crashing down after Hurricane Hugo in 1989, but by the end of the century they had crept back up to a reasonable level. St. Croix real estate is consistently cheaper than St. Thomas. St. John prices are astronomical.

Renters have a fairly broad choice but if they want an ocean view they pay for it, especially in season, when residents have to compete with tourists and snowbirds.

An ideal situation for those unencumbered with families, animals or demanding careers is permanent house-sitting or caretaking for off-islanders who have a house here that they seldom occupy. In this scenario the bachelor or couple lives on the property, often in a palatial house for which they pay nothing. In return they provide usually minimal services for the owner, like watering the plants and mowing the lawn, and have plenty of time left over for their own pursuits, including, if they wish, a full-time job. This is a coveted position, naturally, with the demand much greater than the supply.

I have a friend, Pete Reeves, who lucked into a rent-free situation that has lasted over 10 years. After Hurricane Hugo he was homeless. He was slightly acquainted with a couple from New Jersey who owned an island house that was blown away. However, it had a basement apartment that was habitable after a little fixing up, and he moved in.

Pete was a fastidious squatter and the owners were happy to have someone on the property. He made the apartment quite attractive with furnishings donated by friends or made from hurricane debris. He had gravity-fed water from the cistern and electricity delivered through a series of extension cords from a neighbor's house.

Bearded, pony-tailed, ear-ringed, bikini-clad Pete works as a jack-of-all-trades, but only when he's hungry. Several years after Hugo, when the owners built a new house on the site and put it up for short-term rentals, Pete became the resident caretaker/manager. The guests seem to enjoy meeting a genuine island character and from his point of view it's not very demanding work. He still has time to do odd jobs outside when it's time to pay his tab at the neighborhood bar.

Volunteer Work

Many of the continentals living on St. Croix, including a lot of the snowbirds, give a great deal of time, energy and expertise to one or more of the non-profit organizations that are dependent on volunteers. Some are deeply involved. Many of the service organizations here were founded by continentals. Among the important functions they perform are protecting the environment (St. Croix Environmental Association), preserving the island's heritage (Landmarks Society), caring for stray animals (St. Croix Animal Welfare Center), supporting abused women and children (Women's Coalition of St. Croix) and feeding the homeless (My Brother's Table).

Living in Vacationland

Tourism is the primary "industry" on most Caribbean islands, in some cases the only one. Vacationers love the natural assets of sun, sand and sea and the exotic Caribbean lifestyle. As each island is in competition with all the others, each tries to promote something that makes it distinctive.

While the entire U.S.V.I. is billed as The American Paradise, St. Thomas is best known for duty-free shopping, St. John for its National Park and St. Croix for its unspoiled natural resources, including the third largest barrier reef in the hemisphere, its rich, accessible history, and its mystique as an "undiscovered" gem.

With development on a modest scale, most of the Gentle Virgin's natural beauty, charming ambience and dignity have been preserved. These quiet virtues are a pleasant surprise for discerning visitors and treasured perks for residents.

The inhabitants of St. Croix enjoy the delightful privilege of tourist facilities that are tasteful and low-key: a few understated hotels, none taller than a palm tree; excellent but unpretentious restaurants, a few on the waterfront, many with open-air courtyards; and shops where the sales people are mercifully soft-sell.

Even most of the tourist attractions are upscale, falling into the categories of eco-tourism and/or heritage tourism. These are the main attractions on most visitors' tours.

Whim Museum, a restored sugar estate that interprets the plantation era. Visitors tour a beautiful antique-filled greathouse where the European owners lived and see the three ways sugarcane was pressed: an animal mill, a windmill and a tall steam-producing chimney.

St. George Village Botanical Garden, a 16-acre private park with a comprehensive collection of tropical flora growing in the picturesque ruins of a plantation village.

Buck Island National Monument, a small preserve with a beautiful beach and coral reef a short boat-ride off-shore. Snorkellers follow a marked trail identifying fish and coral species.

"The Wall," a spectacular coral drop-off miles long and hundreds of feet deep that parallels the north shore, one of the best scuba diving sites in the Caribbean.

Carl and Marie Lawaetz Museum, a greathouse in the tropical forest that was the home of a Danish farming family for four generations.

Salt River Bay National Historical Park and Ecological Preserve: A 912-acre site (about two-thirds of it water) on the North Shore that is a park in name only at this writing. This is where Columbus landed and skirmished with the local Indians and where a complete network of tropical ecology thrives in a compact area. Some day, we are promised, the park will have a visitors' center where tourists and residents can learn about the area's extraordinary history and "web of life." Hopefully artifacts that were removed by a Danish archeologist will be returned, including petroglyphs from the ball park where Taino Indians played ritual games.

Point Udall, the easternmost land on U.S. territory, with a monument commemorating the millennium.

Heritage Trail, a driving tour that includes dozens of historical, cultural and natural points of interest all over the island.

Walking tours of historic Christiansted and Frederiksted, including beautiful old churches and townhouses and handsome fortresses.

Guided hikes, horse-back rides, bike rides and kayak tours in areas with both ecological and historical interest.

Southgate Pond Nature Preserve, a bird sanctuary with a salt pond.

St. Croix Aquarium, a delightful small aquarium/marine education center where the fish are borrowed from the surrounding waters for a brief stint in a tank, then returned to their natural habitat.

The "Rainforest," an area of several hundred acres on the west end that is thick with vegetation and officially falls in the category of moist tropical forest. To qualify as a rainforest, much more rainfall is required.

St. Croix LEAP, a wood-working shop in the forest, set among plantation ruins.

Cruzan Rum Factory, where St. Croix's favorite export product is made and sampled.

Divi Carina Bay Casino, a gambling emporium with several gaming tables and scores of slot machines. (In the 1990s the Virgin Islands government voted to allow casino gambling on St. Croix in hopes of jump-starting the ailing economy. The theory was that casinos would lead to the construction of large hotels, increase air traffic, and lure big-spending tourists who would make the economy boom. It didn't happen—yet anyway. In fact, the objective might have back-fired. As of 2001, only one casino has been built, and since it opened in early 2000 it has been filled not by tourists but by locals, many of whom cash their paychecks there and gamble away their earnings.)

Beer-Drinking Pigs at the Domino Club, a thatch-roofed bar in the tropical forest. Since Buster, the original beer-drinking pig, died an alcohol-related death, the proprietor of the bar allows only non-alcoholic beer for Buster's successors. A visitor places an open can of beer in a large pig's cavernous mouth, the pig gulps the liquid and spits out the mangled can. This is a stop on the "cultural tour" offered by the tour busses that transport cruise ship passengers around the island.

Cruise Ships: Only a few call at St. Croix. The harbor in Christiansted, the main town, is too shallow for big ships, and Frederiksted has no harbor, just a pier jutting into the open sea. Although the government pours millions after millions into enlarging and upgrading that pier, St. Croix will, thankfully, never be competitive with St. Thomas. There the excellent big harbor accommodates up to 10 ships a day, each with thousands of passengers who overwhelm the small island and the duty-free shops on Main Street.

The Season

Although the temperature here is near perfect year around, winter is the time most tourists flock to the tropics to escape harsh weather up north. The Tourist Season officially extends from December 15 to April 15, when airline and hotel rates are highest and when the many residents who are dependent on tourism make most of their income for the year. Those four months are known as The Tourist Season, The Season, High Season, In Season or simply Season.

Dress Optional

Continentals in the Virgin Islands dress for the climate and easy living in clothes that are cool, comfortable and casual. Shorts, T-shirts and sandals are almost a uniform, for both sexes, and it's possible to live in them night and day, year around.

For many the outfit is a statement. Their down-graded wardrobes reflect their choice of a simpler, more informal lifestyle. I know women who vow never to wear stockings again and men who refuse to own a jacket and tie.

Most of us will dress up slightly when we go out in the evening. The men may switch to long pants and sport shirts, the women to skirts, dresses or pants. But even when we females are at our dressiest, we still don't look anywhere near as elegant as the local women do on their way to the office.

West Indians and Hispanics are far more formal, more fashionable, more dignified in their dress than mainlanders are. Many local women go to work in linen dresses or suits, hose and high heels. Older women, especially those from down-island, are never seen in pants, always a dress and usually a hat.

Almost everyone wears American-style clothes, except for cultural events. The exceptions include robes worn from head to toe by some of the Muslim women (others wear head covers with jeans); African dashikis and caftans, expressing pride of heritage more often than place of origin; the knitted caps that contain voluminous dreadlocks; and *guayaberas,* the cool, pleated, embroidered shirts that are considered formal enough to replace men's jackets on Hispanic islands but are surprisingly rare here. (I'm told *guayaberas* were very popular in the 1970s, even with trendy teenagers.)

On Sundays many of the locals dress for church in elaborate finery. Women and girls wear silks, chiffons and taffetas. Despite the tropical heat, many men wear suits, even three-piece suits. The continentals who go to church in their island attire look like they're from a different planet.

Still, on Sunday or any day, they look a lot better than many of the tourists, especially cruise ship passengers, who often are dressed for the beach even if they're in town. Apparently they don't stop to think that in this culture their exposed bodies might be offensive.

When I was cruising I discovered that the least developed islands could have the most stringent taboos and it was always a good idea for visitors to dress conservatively. The Pacific islands were a big surprise, considering the scantily-clad natives. There were islands where all the women were topless but it was taboo for them to expose their lower torsos. They covered up even when they bathed in the sea, wearing their sarongs right into the water. And they frowned on visitors who exposed their thighs.

The Pacific islanders are indigenous people who have nurtured their customs for centuries. The younger Caribbean culture is much freer, certainly concerning dress.

The American islands are probably the least formal of all—one more reason I, a barefoot hippie at heart, feel so at home.

National Dress

The national dress throughout the Caribbean, including the V.I., is madras plaid, made into short-sleeve shirts for men and long skirts and elaborate headdresses for women. These brightly-colored costumes were adopted in the last century. They are worn especially for dancing the quadrille, a dignified rather solemn dance adapted by enslaved Africans from the court dancing performed by their masters in the plantation era. The hats indicate the wearer's status by the number of starched, upright points: a woman wearing one point is single, two points is married and three points is divorced or widowed—and available.

Driving in the Left Lane

Driving on the left side of the road in cars designed to drive on the right is an adventure almost unique to the U.S. Virgin Islands. Since most of the roads are narrow and winding two-laners, the driver, who is on the left-hand side of the car, must pull out into the lane of oncoming traffic to see if he can pass.

Absurd? Senseless? Insane? The bizarre custom is so characteristic of local idiosyncracies it's become both a symbol of and metaphor for island style. In St. Croix, Life in the Left Lane is a slogan we flaunt on T-shirts and bumper stickers.

Why do the people in this American territory drive on the left? Probably because that's how the British did it long ago, and no one has taken the trouble to change it. There is almost universal agreement that it is a ridiculous and dangerous practice, yet as late as 2001 there is little pressure to correct it.

As it is, newcomers to the islands are thrown into confusion or even panic by the unexpected need to Think Left. Vacationers here for relaxation must shift into anxiety mode as soon as they get behind the wheel. If they lose their concentration for a moment they might stray into oncoming traffic. If something unexpected happens while driving, their automatic reactions are the opposite of what they should be. Night driving is a nightmare because headlights aimed for the side of the road stateside shine right in the eyes of oncoming drivers here.

Miraculously, fatal head-on collisions are infrequent.

A really scary consequence of the system is that the taxi-vans which provide most of our public transportation pick up and discharge passengers through a right-hand door, in the middle of the road. They stop anywhere they are hailed, and often there is no place to pull off to the side. I'm happy to say that school buses and public buses introduced in the late 1990s were designed with doors on the left.

By tropical standards, public transportation vehicles in the Virgin Islands are dull and ordinary.

On other islands, most famously Haiti and the Philippines, where buses and vans dominate traffic, their decoration is a delightful folk art and vehicles are completely camouflaged with bright images of island life. The buses transport both passengers and cargo and are very picturesque when stuffed inside and out with animated people and chickens, banana stalks and lumpy sacks of produce for the market.

In the relatively sophisticated U.S.V.I. only a few van owners express their individuality and then only by names painted on the rear mud flaps. Sweet Lips is my favorite. Biblical references such as The Good Shepherd are common, interspersed with secular suggestions such as Get Down on It and Come Fly with Me. One local van makes a common Caribbean boast, No Problem, while another complains of Lots of Problem.

The best thing about driving on St. Croix, aside from the beautiful scenery, is sharing the road with the world's most courteous, considerate drivers. The men who drive slow heavy equipment pull off to the side frequently to let the cars piled up behind them pass. No one ever waits long on a side road before someone waves him into the traffic on the main road, flicking headlights or tapping the horn as a signal to proceed. When someone does something wrong or stupid, there is never a loud angry chorus of honks. Horns are used sparingly. In fact they are most frequently used to say Hi to a passing friend or to acknowledge a courteous act by another driver—and then with just a couple of light taps.

Hitchhikers here have an unusual style. They don't signal with their thumbs. Instead they stand immobile by the side of the road until a car is alongside, when they suddenly shout out their destinations, calling "Christiansted!" (a town) or "Sunny Isle!" (a shopping center) or simply "Ride!" It was quite a relief when I finally comprehended that whatever they were hollering it was not "Yankee Go Home!"

Emy Thomas

Palm Trees

Feathery palm fronds
caressed by balmy breezes
ripple in delight

Building a Dream House

For outsiders relocating to a tropical island, having a home with a fabulous ocean view is often a major component of the plan. Paradise is where we buy or build our dream houses.

Most sensible people buy a house that's already built, knowing that the normal hassle of building is compounded here by the frustration of working on island time and the curious contortions of doing business in the left lane.

Buying is also likely to be cheaper. As I write in 2001, residential construction on St. Croix costs between $150 and $250 per square foot. It is higher on St. Thomas and highest on St. John.

Despite the negatives, a surprising number of people go ahead and build anyway. I understand. For some of us houses are an emotional, very personal thing, and no amount of logic can convince us that anything but our own design will do.

When I was ready to acquire a dream house on St. Croix I was disappointed to find that nothing on the market came close to my ideal. I had very definite ideas of what I wanted—small and simple with a West Indian look. None of the available houses could be coaxed into that description.

Despite the dire warnings about building on the island, especially as a single woman, that I would lose my mind and my shirt, I was determined to have my dream house. When I found a lot just under an acre with a view embracing a tranquil bay, a reef with gently-breaking surf and the multi-colored Caribbean Sea, I knew that was it. I was sure that view would keep me happy, and I was right.

My dream house was apparently meant to be. Although I knew nothing about building a house when I arrived on the island, I moved into mine less than a year later.

I knew only two people on St. Croix when I made the move, Tinker Bell Riggs and Leo Levi. They were great friends and did everything possible to help my dream come true. They gave me a temporary home on their boat, they gave me a job, and they introduced me to everyone they knew who might help my project, including Barry Allaire, a young builder just starting his own company, who became my contractor. He made the process so pleasant we are still friends.

I love the look of traditional West Indian houses. Usually made of wood, painted in bright colors and trimmed with delightful gingerbread, they have hip roofs and small doors and windows fitted with two sets of shutters (no glass), louvered inside for everyday use and solid outside for storms. They are picturesque but dark and airless inside. I need light and cooling breezes.

With the help of an architect/friend in Puerto Rico, Chauncey ("Laurie") Williams, I designed a small building with the hip roof and basic simplicity of a Caribbean house but more open to the climate and the view. A large gallery (as we call porches here) spans the front of the house, facing the prevailing easterlies and the view. A central greatroom and two bedrooms, one on each side, open to the gallery through French doors, and I let the tradewinds blow through.

The exterior is pink and the roof is "tin." Like almost every contemporary house in the V.I. it is constructed of concrete block. (This, incidentally, is an ideal material for people building island style—a little at a time, as cash is available. Some houses take years to complete, with progress measured literally block by concrete block.)

If I say so myself, mine is the perfect little tropical house. If I did it over again now, the only things I would change are hurricane-related: storm shutters that are an integral part of the design, the strongest roof available, and a storm shelter under the foundation where my dogs and I could take refuge if the roof blew off anyway.

The V.I. was not storm-conscious when I built in 1986. By the turn of the century, after four hurricanes in a decade and at least a decade more of intense storm activity predicted, a dream house must be a fortress too.

I'd like to pass along some observations for property shoppers. Higher elevations are breezier and less buggy than low sites. Appliances and electronic equipment have a shorter lifespan in waterfront homes where salt and moisture are always in the air. Homes on hilltops are more likely to be blown away in a hurricane, while those near sea level are in jeopardy from the storm surge accompanying hurricanes. And be aware that the V.I. is on a fault-line. In 1867 an earthquake and tidal wave did considerable damage to St. Croix. No catastrophic quake has occurred since, but there are small tremors recorded all the time.

Home Is Where the Boat Is

A boat can be a floating home and is an appealing option in the tropics. "Live aboards" can change their location at will. They can tie up to a dock in a marina, plug in and enjoy all the conveniences of life ashore, or they can swing on a mooring in a harbor, catch the tradewinds and the views, enjoy privacy and the pleasure of jumping over the side for a swim. It's an unusual lifestyle that I enjoyed for many years and wrote about in another book, *Home Is Where the Boat Is*.

The worst part of owning a boat in the tropics is their vulnerability in hurricanes. Their mortality rate is high even in a minor hurricane, even when well-secured in a marina or one of the most protected anchorages—the so-called "hurricane holes." They are subjected to colossal winds blowing from more than one direction, tremendous tidal surges, the "fetch" of wave action in shallow depths, and ramming by other boats that have broken loose.

Insurance for boats in the tropics is understandably high. In 2001, the premium for a typical live-aboard boat (a 35-foot fiberglass sloop seven to ten years old, worth about $125,000) is about $2,500. Not all boat owners make the investment.

One solution is to go north or south, out of the hurricane belt, for the storm season. Some insurance companies require that of vessels they cover. But for boat owners without that mobility, all they can do when a hurricane threatens is secure the boat as best they can and pray. Some stay aboard in the belief they can do something if the craft is threatened. There are cases of owners saving the boat by revving the engine into the wind or fending off other boats but there are also cases in which both the boat and owner are lost. St. Thomas had several fatalities in Hurricane Marilyn, all of them boaters who had elected to stay aboard.

The most radical decision when confronted with an approaching hurricane is to go to sea, hoping to sail out of the storm's path or, if necessary, to ride it out. The strategy <u>can</u> work, but too often the boat and the people aboard are never seen again.

Hurricanes Happen

Getting Ready

Hurricanes are a terrifying aspect of life in the tropics and, thanks to global warming, they're getting more and more frequent.

In the 15 years I've lived in the Virgin Islands, we've been hit four times—in 1989 by Hugo, officially a Category IV hurricane, unofficially a V (the worst there is); by Marilyn in '95, a Category II (unofficially a III); Georges, a II, in '98; and Lenny, another IV, in '99.

Hugo just about wiped out St. Croix; Marilyn did the same to St. Thomas; Georges scared us to death approaching as a Category IV going on V but, miraculously, it dwindled to a II just before hitting the Virgin Islands and did relatively little damage. In 1999 the season was almost over when Hurricane Lenny came out of left field—literally. Instead of the usual formation in the Atlantic, Lenny started in the Caribbean and headed east. By the time it approached St. Croix it was another terrifying Category IV likely to become a V. Luckily the eye stayed just off-shore through most of its passage, crossing only the southeastern tip of the island. We felt winds over 100 miles an hour but amazingly, there was little damage.

September is the month when most storms happen in the Caribbean, but there's a possibility six months out of every

48

year. Hurricane Season runs from June 1 through November 30, when one tropical wave after another forms off Africa and marches westward across the Atlantic. Many tropical waves ultimately dissipate or go north or south; others arrive at the islands as harmless rainstorms. But almost every year there is at least one that increases in strength.

When a wave is upgraded to a tropical depression, our anxiety level rises and we start checking our emergency supplies. If it intensifies further to a tropical storm bearing a name, we raid the stores for kerosene lamps and candles, flashlight and radio batteries, canned food and drinking water. If it makes the dreaded leap to a hurricane, we go into crisis mode and prepare for the worst. We usually have at least a day to get ready.

Obviously anything that can be blown away is secured or brought inside, and then the house or apartment is dressed for battle. By now most of us have acquired "hurricane shutters" to cover windows and glass doors. These range from scraps of plywood to heavy-duty roll-down doors like those securing store-fronts. There are also traditional wooden shutters, aluminum or plastic panels in tracks, and aluminum accordion doors. Because tightly-enclosed structures can implode in a storm, it's recommended to crack some shuttered windows to equalize the pressure from without.

Before I had shutters I spent hours packing my possessions away in closets and cupboards. Even if there wasn't structural damage, enough rain and salt spray and mud and leaves came through the windows and under the doors to damage whatever was exposed. The shutters keep the house wonderfully clean and dry but since they don't guarantee that the roof will stay on, I still stash away my most precious belongings—paintings and books, my laptop computer and diskettes—to help insure their survival. It's also recommended to put ID, money and insurance papers in ziploc bags. These I put in the clothes dryer, my hurricane safe.

As we make our preparations we hope and pray the storm will turn away or fizzle out. If it doesn't, we seek refuge, either at official emergency shelters in schools or churches, in our own homes or someone else's, wherever we feel safe.

For my first hurricane, in my carefree youth in San Juan, I went to a bar and listened to my favorite entertainer sing "Stormy Weather" and other appropriate songs. Luckily the threatened storm never materialized. Now that I've been through a few, I know a hurricane is not a good excuse for a party and I soberly go to the only place I feel really secure—underground. I wish I had thought to build a shelter under my foundation. Since I didn't, I (and my three dogs) impose on friends who have apartments under their homes.

Why don't we get off the island? Most of us are so attached to our homes and gardens we wouldn't dream of abandoning them. Although there's not much we can do during the storm, it's important to pick up the pieces immediately after to save what's left. By patching broken windows we can keep out thieves and further rain and wind; by propping up fallen trees and shrubs we can often get them to re-root.

Besides, hurricanes are so unpredictable we don't know for sure whether a storm is going to hit us, or how hard, until the last minute. By then it's too late. The airport is closed and the sea is too rough for any ship or boat to venture out. If we did decide to leave ahead of time, chances are the hurricane would go elsewhere—and maybe even follow us.

Survival Stories

A hurricane is a historic milestone for everyone who survives it. On St. Croix we date everything in our lives pre- or post-Hugo. For many victims, life was never the same again.

Everyone who lives through a killer hurricane has a dramatic story to tell—and everyone loves to tell it, *ad infinitum*. For months after Hurricane Hugo, it was hard to find anyone on St. Croix who could talk about anything else.

Hugo hit St. Croix the night of September 17-18, 1989. The island had not had a major hurricane for 60 years and many of us hadn't a clue how to prepare, physically or mentally.

The forecast was terrifying enough—140-knot winds. When the storm stalled over the island, raging for 12 hours and spawning tornadoes over 200 miles an hour, ripping off roofs and knocking down houses, many people were sure they were going to die.

My story is gratefully tame. My friend Tinker, my dog Benji (the only pet I had at the time) and I rested comfortably on a king-size bed in the small apartment under Tinker's house. Her partner Leo had died the year before and we were glad to have each other's company.

51

We heard the winds build up, louder and louder, until something like a freight train roared by, filling our heads with terrible pressure. That was a tornado, we later learned, and there were several of them during that endless night.

We heard horrendous crashes, bangs and thumps above us. From our sanctuary below the foundation we couldn't interpret what the noises signified but it was quite clear that Tinker's house was tumbling down, slowly, slowly. We were frightened, of course, but we stayed dry and warm throughout the storm and we felt reasonably confident we were not in personal danger.

We did worry, however, about three friends who had stayed upstairs on the main floor of the house. We learned later that as the roof tore off, piece by piece, and the concrete-block walls crumbled, chunk by chunk, and the furniture and appliances flew around, they moved from room to room through ever-increasing piles of debris. Ultimately they decided a small closet was their only hope. The three stood in the cramped space the rest of the night, taking turns at gripping the small louvers, desperately trying to hold the doors shut against the onslaught of wind.

They survived and, incredibly, so did everyone else on the island. Many were in closets, some were under beds, some in shower stalls. I know a few people who tried to squeeze into bathroom cabinets when there was nothing else left; their heads were protected but their butts weren't.

Those left with no place to hide grabbed anything that might protect them from flying debris: a mattress or pillow, a shower curtain or piece of rubble. My friend Geri Overton was in her pantry when her roof blew off. She spent the next few hours with a frying pan on her head, the only thing between her and the maelstrom swirling around her.

There were several stories of people retreating to cisterns, standing in a few feet of water for the remainder of the storm. Others made a dash to cars where they prayed they wouldn't be crushed or blown away. The few boaters who chose to stay aboard their vessels had some wild rides. One small trimaran flipped over a couple of times before fetching up ashore with its owner only slightly bruised from the surrealistic somersaults.

As the winds abated in the morning and we ventured out, we found the entire island virtually destroyed. It looked like Hiroshima after the atomic bomb. Every building was damaged if not demolished. All leaves had been stripped from trees, all green had been sucked from vegetation, leaving a brown wasteland strewn with rubble and debris. Sheets of metal roofing, called "galvanize" in Crucian, had sliced through cars and wrapped around trees. Furniture and appliances dotted the landscape far from any home. Boats littered the shoreline, tossed helter-skelter.

The roads were blocked with fallen telephone poles and trees. Among the volunteers helping to clear pathways were many able-bodied men wielding machetes, the islands' all-purpose cutting tool. The activity, absolutely normal to anyone who lives here, was misinterpreted by stateside visitors as "natives rioting!"

We did have looting, but there was no violence involved. The stores had been so badly damaged there was no need to break in. One simply walked in through a hole in the wall, took what one wanted and left.

The only store that wasn't looted in the chaotic few days before Uncle Sam sent in the Army was a large supermarket whose Arab owners stood on the roof, armed with assault weapons, and threatened to shoot anyone who attempted to enter the store.

As a consequence of the Hugo looting, curfews were imposed for each subsequent storm, even when there was little damage. They are good for keeping sightseers off the roads so that repairmen can work, but they need to be modified so that people with legitimate reasons to be out—such as checking on an elderly parent or a business—can do so.

After Hugo, the roads from Tinker's ruined house to mine were impassable for two days. When I was finally able to inch my way around obstacles, the devastation I passed was so total I didn't dare hope my house would still be standing. I had to walk the last half mile and as I rounded a bend and saw my roof I was so overcome with relief I sat down in the middle of the road and cried.

I was one of the few people on the island with a habitable home. The gallery roof was gone and the front of the house was smashed—French doors and louvered windows were broken or missing—but my main roof, although it had lifted, was still on. And that was so much more than most people had I felt undeservedly, guiltily, blessed.

For many of us the hurricane was a spiritual experience. Whatever doubts and loss of faith we had during the night of terror and the subsequent sight of our devastated island, they were quickly offset by the news that no one was killed. A few deaths in the next few days were indirectly related to the hurricane, but no one was killed outright by the storm itself. There were not even many injuries. It seemed miraculous, a gift from God within a catastrophic act of God. Despite the destruction and terrible material losses, "Thank God for life" was a mantra heard everywhere.

I was surprised to discover how much I cherished everyone—not just my friends but also the boy who helped me with gardening, the neighbors who stopped by to see if I was all right, even the surly clerk at the convenience store. Our common survival was a marvel and a bond. With each familiar face I ran into there was a rush of affection and a hug. For me Hugo became synonymous with hugs.

The Long Recovery

On a small island far from civilization, recovery can take months, sometimes years, and can be more traumatic than the actual storm. Damage is calculated in physical terms—buildings destroyed, lives lost—but there is a tremendous toll on human psyches as well. Each storm is followed by an exodus of residents who are homeless and/or jobless and/or unable or unwilling to cope with devastation or the threat of it anymore.

When a hurricane hits the mainland, recovery starts immediately. Emergency crews rush in from neighboring cities and states to assist in the clean-up. Roads are cleared within hours, electricity and telephones are restored within days, and buildings are repaired within weeks.

On an island where the entire population has been impacted and the infrastructure is just about totaled, local emergency personnel are overwhelmed and we must wait for outside help to be organized and transported across the ocean by ship or plane—workers as well as their supplies, vehicles and equipment.

Meanwhile, we live under tarpaulins surrounded by debris and without essential services for weeks or·even months. It sounds incredible but after Hugo I went for six months without electricity and five months without a phone. Recovery has improved with each successive hurricane, but generators and cellular phones are still considered necessities by those who can afford them.

After Hugo our heroes were the telephone and electricity crews who came from all over the world and toiled for months to get us wired again. We even had one martyr—Pedro Cepeda from Guam, who died when he fell from a utility pole. The villains were the contractor/swindlers who took advantage of the chaos and the desperate need of homeless people and collected big money for little or no work.

A lot of construction workers came from the states. There was plenty of work and good pay. The carpetbaggers seemed to run to type; pick-up trucks full of loud, beer-swilling, pony-tailed, tank-topped, pot-bellied white guys is one of the abiding post-Hugo images. We were grateful for the work they did but, unfortunately, many of them didn't fit into our ethnically diverse society and racial tension was high.

Getting the money to pay for rebuilding was an all-consuming chore. FEMA (The Federal Emergency Management Administration) set up shop right away, giving or lending small amounts to people without insurance and supplying big cobalt-blue tarps to replace lost roofs. (The color has entered V.I. vocabulary as FEMA Blue.)

Those with insurance waited for imported claims adjusters to make the rounds. Then we waited for a settlement. Then we waited for a check. For some of us the check never came, as a few insurance companies went belly-up in the wake of this unprecedented disaster. The good news was the V.I. government accepted responsibility for the companies' failures; they should not have been licensed without proper co-insurance. It took four years to get all the money owed us but, considering the condition of the territory, we were thankful and a little surprised to get any.

There are still a few Hugo ruins blemishing the landscape. The owners could not afford to rebuild or they took their insurance money and left. For a few years after the storm the most common real estate ad was SLAB WITH A VIEW. When the slabs were cleared of rubble, often the only indication that anyone had ever lived there was a toilet securely fastened to the floor—a throne indeed.

Now we've been through so many storms we're getting good at it. After Hugo and Marilyn, the local building code was stiffened so effectively (requiring metal "hurricane clips" and straps to join roofs to walls; screws instead of nails in roofs; and a shorter distance between rafters) that Georges in 1998 caused hardly any structural damage. To be sure Georges was a much less severe storm, but still the winds were well over 100 knots and could have been quite destructive. What a relief it was to look out when it was all over and see that most buildings were intact. FEMA was so impressed it called the V.I. a role model of hazard mitigation. It was quite a treat for this territory, normally ridiculed for its left lane style, to be applauded for doing something right.

The improvements might ultimately relieve insurance exploitation as well. Windstorm insurance rates are high in the V.I., and after each hurricane they zoom up some more. The annual homeowners' premium for my little house, based on $170,000 replacement cost, is almost $3,000. I know people who have been quoted up to $15,000. If they don't have a mortgage, which requires insurance, many owners simply don't buy a policy and take their chances on being able to afford whatever repairs might be necessary. They "self-insure."

Given all the physical and financial distress of living in a hurricane belt, a logical question is why does anyone do it? Aside from the fact that it's paradise and we love it, is any place perfect? Consider California with earthquakes, the Midwest and floods, the South and tornadoes, the northwest and forest fires. If I have to live under the threat of a natural disaster, I'll choose hurricanes. At least they come with advance warning, giving us time to prepare, physically and mentally.

Jump Up

Caribbean culture (kulcha as we say in Crucian) is colorful and joyful. Music and dance are its heart. Despite the appalling heritage of slavery, West Indians are basically a fun-loving people and their happy, rhythmic music, whether reggae, salsa, calypso, soca or quelbe, is full of a contagious *joie de vivre*. It's hard to be with a group of West Indians and not have a good time yourself.

Annual carnivals are the supreme manifestation of every island's popular culture but in between there are numerous reasons to "Jump Up." That's the apt name for a party in the Virgin Islands.

"Cultural" entertainment that caters to tourists usually features limbo dancing, a broken bottle dancer and a fire eater. According to Wayne James, a Crucian cultural historian, these awesome acts were probably developed by the enslaved: Limbo dancing could celebrate their survival of the narrow confines of the slave ships' holds; dancing in bare feet on broken glass and opening their mouths to flaming torches might show their defiance of the pain inflicted by their masters' whips.

Other regular performers at cultural events in the V.I. are mocko jumbies, steel bands, scratch bands and quadrille dancers.

Mocko jumbies are stilt dancers representing African spirits. According to centuries-old West African beliefs, they are spiritual guardians of the people, protecting them from evil spirits. Mysteriously disguised in colorful costumes and masks, they tower above spectators on stilts up to 20 feet high as they dance and kick and perform amazing feats of balance. In the U.S.V.I. they are the highlight of any cultural event.

Thanks to a few dedicated teachers who preserved the tradition when it was on the verge of extinction, there are many young mocko jumbies in training, assuring a continuing supply of this charismatic cultural icon.

The music they dance to is provided by scratch bands (also called scratchy or fungi bands) or steel bands.

Like scratch bands anywhere, the local ones are delightfully inventive and include several home-made instruments such as banjos made from tin cans; horns made from car exhaust pipes; drums made from logs and animal skin; flutes of bamboo; and rhythm instruments made of dried gourds and pods. The name scratchy band probably came from the *guiro*, a dried gourd with ridges that are scraped with a wire pick to make a scratching sound.

Two indigenous forms of music they play, calypso and quelbe, date back to colonial times. Calypso is an updated version of caiso, a slave-invented method of sending messages and commentary in song. Quelbe is the music that accompanies quadrille, a Creole dance based on the formal minuet-style routines that were performed by the white folks in plantation greathouses.

The music that really defines the Caribbean is the distinctively mellow, resonant sound of the popular steel bands. They usually play calypso, naturally, but they are marvelously adaptable to any type of music. There are thrilling steel band renditions of marches, hymns, symphonies and jazz.

The bands are comprised of many steel "pans" or "drums," all made from 55-gallon oil cans. The pitch of the drum (tenor, bass, alto, etc.) is determined by how deep the top is "sunk," and specific notes spanning several octaves are created by hollows hammered into the top. The pans are drummed with mallets.

The steel pan is the only new musical instrument developed anywhere in the world in the 20th Century. Trinidad is the originator and still the premier producer of pans, but they have been embraced throughout the region. They are the cultural symbol of every island in the Caribbean.

In the U.S.V.I. almost every child has an opportunity to become a pan player by joining a steel band at school, church or a youth group. And almost every child does.

Reef Fish

Who would believe fish
colored like rainbows swimming
in a turquoise sea?

Carnival!

Carnival is the ultimate Caribbean event. Almost every island in the West Indies has one—a big, colorful annual festival that is an occasion for cultural pride and celebration and an excuse to carouse and let go.

Even before emancipation, Caribbean people found reasons for revelry. Today's carnival has evolved from plantation-era celebrations and combines traditions of West African masquerades (costumes, masks, queens and mocko jumbies) with European festivals (kings and queens, music and dancing).

Carnival in the V.I. is a weeks-long season of partying and pageantry, all leading up to a climactic parade featuring elaborately-costumed celebrants in troupes and floupes (troupes accompanied by floats) dancing down the streets to the pounding beat of highly amplified steel bands repeatedly playing calypso tunes newly composed for the occasion.

"Parade" is a misnomer when describing this event. Except for a token military presence and young drum majorettes at the beginning of the parade, nobody "marches." Instead the adults prance, dance, gyrate and bump-and-grind as they slowly proceed through the streets, frequently joined by spectators who get carried away and dance along.

63

Carnival is a Bacchanal, well lubricated by island rum. There are religious themes—Christian and pagan—but carnival is basically a secular event, loud and raunchy. The names of troupes include Fun, Intrigue, Road Party and Clear De Road. The wildly colorful costumes are made of shiny fabrics, spangles and glitter, beads, fringe, and feathers, feathers, feathers. They range from skimpy bikinis to huge, elaborate constructions that radiate from the wearer and are so heavy and cumbersome they are mounted on wheels that he or she pulls and pushes through the streets. Some of these costumes are so intricate they take all year to make.

Trinidad's carnival is generally considered the best in the islands, right up there with New Orleans and Rio de Janeiro and, like those, it is a celebration of Mardi Gras, the last chance to live it up before the somber six weeks of Christian Lent. On other islands carnivals fall throughout the year.

In the U.S.V.I., each of the three main islands has its own version of Carnival, thoughtfully spread throughout the year so that everyone in the territory can participate in all three Bacchanals if they so choose.

St. Croix starts the carousing with the Crucian Christmas Festival, which begins in mid-December with pageants to choose a queen and prince and princess, calypso competitions and band concerts. The Festival culminates in four events—and four unofficial holidays for government workers: a Food Fair; J'Ouvert, an early-morning "tramp" through the streets by steel and brass bands and their followers; a children's parade; and finally the climactic happening, the adults' parade. This is held on the Saturday closest to January 6, Epiphany or Three Kings Day. Running simultaneously with the main events is the Festival Village, a fair grounds offering food and drink, rides and games, and nightly entertainment.

In St. Thomas, the Virgin Islands Carnival is held in April, after Easter. It ranks very high on the carnival charts, probably a close second to Trinidad. St. John holds its Carnival the first weekend in July, conveniently tied in with two holidays, V.I. Emancipation Day on the 3rd and U.S. Independence Day on the 4th. In case anyone still wants to "play mas" (masquerade), he can pop over to the British Virgin Islands the next month for a three-day carnival called Summer Fest.

No wonder Herman Wouk chose the title *Don't Stop the Carnival* for his classic novel about life in the islands. A carnival figured only marginally in his story, but Wouk used it as a symbol of and metaphor for Caribbean life—colorful and carefree but underlaid with a mysterious primitive streak.

Incidentally, almost every island in the Caribbean claims to be the setting for Wouk's delightful story. Although he had a home on St. Thomas and has lived on a couple of other islands, his fictional island is probably a composite of several locales.

Emy Thomas

Rainbows for Breakfast

Sapphires and emeralds tumble in the Caribbean Sea,
jade and turquoise lick the shore,
garnets define the horizon.

A morning shower swipes the ocean jewels,
the sun aligns them with amber, amethyst and rubies
and flings them across the sky.

Holidays in Heaven

The Virgin Islands has more legal holidays than anywhere else under the U.S. flag—22 of them, 11 federal and 11 local. Up until the year 2000 they were all days off with pay for "non-essential" employees of the territorial government. That year the governor bowed to an ongoing financial crisis by removing four dates from the paid holiday category and thereby "saving" millions of dollars in unearned wages.

A third of the working population in the V.I. is employed by the local government, and one of the perks that makes a government job popular is so many holidays. It's rare to work a month without at least one three-day weekend.

The local holidays reveal a lot about Island Style.

January 6 **Three Kings Day.** This holiday, commemorating the visit to the baby Jesus by the Three Kings, or Three Wise Men, or Magi, is a double whammy on St. Croix; the island's carnival, the Crucian Christmas Festival, culminates with the adults' parade on the Saturday closest to Three Kings Day. For children in the large Hispanic population, Three Kings is better than Christmas. This is the day gifts are given.

March or April **Holy Thursday, Good Friday, and Easter Monday** are all official local holidays, making Easter a five-day weekend. Camping out is an Easter tradition that was started by Puerto Ricans and has been adopted by West

Indians. Families and friends gather together on their favorite beach, set up tents and tarpaulins, plywood and "galvanize" shanties, cots, tables, chairs, stoves, coolers, refrigerators, TVs, stereos, amplifiers and, of course, generators, for a non-stop party.

July 3 **Emancipation Day.** In 1848 on this day the sounds of conch shell horns and African drums summoned slaves from plantations all over the island to converge on the fort in Frederiksted. There a man called Buddhoe led thousands of enslaved Africans in a peaceful confrontation with the Danish Governor, Peter Von Scholten. The sympathetic governor declared all slaves in the Danish West Indies free, an action for which he was recalled to Denmark in disgrace. Today Frederiksted is proudly called Freedom City.

November 1 **Liberty Day** honors a distinguished native son, D. Hamilton Jackson, an early 20th century labor leader, judge and journalist. The day is also known as Bull and Bread Day, because a bull is slaughtered and roasted over an open fire.

December 26 **Christmas Second Day** Like Easter Monday, this is a day-after holiday provided by a thoughtful government for recovery purposes. It might have started as Boxing Day when the British were in power. Christmas in the tropics is a rather schizophrenic affair, with northern traditions celebrated alongside strictly local customs. Hence Santa Claus arrives at a children's party by boat or jet-skis, and eggnog is served at an adult party along with homemade guavaberry wine. In the old days "Christmas trees" were either inkberry trees with candles skewered on the thorns or dried century plant stalks festooned with hand-made ornaments, both quite lovely. But since the invention of refrigerated containers, pine and fir trees from northern climes have been shipped to the islands and have supplanted the local trees in popularity. Most people decorate them just like in the states, with electric lights, colored balls and tinsel, but there are also distinctive island ornaments made of shells, beach glass and other local ingredients.

The four dates that were eliminated as paid holidays for government workers but are still observed are:

March 31 **Transfer Day**, commemorating the sale of the Virgin Islands from Denmark to the U.S. in 1917.

Third Monday in June **Organic Act Day**, marking ratification of the V.I. constitution.

Fourth Monday in July and third Monday in October **Hurricane Supplication Day** and **Hurricane Thanksgiving Day**. These holidays have no relation to the beginning and end of the hurricane season as established by the U.S. Weather Service, June 1 and November 30. Instead we pray for deliverance almost two months after the official start of the season and give thanks for being spared six weeks before the season is over. The dates were chosen by the clergy as far back as 1726, long before the Weather Service came along, and reflect the beliefs of this local ditty:

> *June, too soon.*
> *July, stand by.*
> *August, don't trust.*
> *September, remember.*
> *October, all over.*

A few notes on national holidays:

The New Year is celebrated here much as in the rest of the world except that islanders call it Old Year Night, not New Year's Eve.

Christopher Columbus is not a hero to many here, because of his lack of humanitarianism toward indigenous peoples and the slave trade resulting from his discoveries. The V.I. has given Columbus Day another identity as Puerto Rico/U.S.V.I. Friendship Day.

Another local curiosity is St. Patrick's Day which, though not a holiday, has a surprising niche on the St. Croix calendar. There has been a parade every year since 1968 on the Saturday nearest March 17, with whites and blacks alike awash in green, reveling in "being Irish for a day." Many West Indians have Irish ancestry and Irish names and are Catholics. For them Patrick is an especially meaningful saint because he was once enslaved.

Precious Metals

Full moon rises gold
and slowly turns to silver
as copper sun dawns

Household Pests

I share my open screen-less house with many uninvited creatures—cockroaches and wasps, centipedes and millipedes, grasshoppers and beetles, frogs and rodents. I trade off their presence for the joy of wide open doors and windows, where the balmy breezes blow through and nothing screens the gorgeous view.

In the V.I. I'm happy to say we don't have any really vicious household pests like poisonous spiders. Worm-like millipedes (locally called gongolos) secrete an acid that burns, and centipedes have a nasty bite, but neither is life-threatening. The most dangerous visitor I can think of is a repulsive toad with the French name of *crapaud* (appropriately pronounced crapo) that exudes a poison that can kill a small animal. Luckily they are rare.

Mice, rats and frogs are the most serious household adversaries in the V.I.

The tree frogs that sometimes congregate at my house are dirty, slimy little beasts. They lurk all over the house, especially in the moist bathrooms, dribbling large squishy blobs of smelly excrement down the walls and over the floor and then walking right through it! They leap out of vases when I empty flowers, they materialize from under boxes when I move things and they hide under toilet rims, from whence they launch counter-attacks when bombarded by human waste. If they get into the cistern they croak ecstatically, especially at night. The cistern is the concrete water tank under the house. It makes a great echo chamber.

My favorite frog story concerns two plumbers, big brawny West Indian men, who came to fix my leaking toilet. As the boss removed the cover of the tank, a frog leapt out. He dropped the cover and they both jumped and shrieked like young girls. Those macho men wouldn't go back into the bathroom until I, the helpless female, disposed of the frog. They fixed my toilet that day but have never returned to my house. Whenever I call for a plumber they send someone else.

The field mice we have here are adorable and delightfully acrobatic little critters. I've seen them swing from wires like Tarzan and chin themselves like Kilroy. But they are amazingly destructive. Those tiny little teeth have dined on everything from my fruit to my watercolor paintings and best clothes. Luckily my dogs enjoy hunting mice and they usually manage to dispatch them before too much is destroyed.

I've been in the tropics and lived in an open house long enough to be quite nonchalant about most critters, but I doubt that I'll ever be cool about rats.

For years I had an electric stove with a fatal attraction for rats. Every few months a repulsive rodent disappeared into the guts of the appliance, tearing out the insulation, then chewing the wires and electrocuting itself. I didn't know it was there until it started to smell. I had to remove numerous nuts and bolts and panels before I could extricate the stinking body. It was a gross, grisly operation.

Since I replaced that stove and a friend had the brilliant idea of screening all the openings on the new stove, my rat encounters are much less traumatic. I still hate the creatures but nothing, not even the possibility of a visit by a dreaded rat, is enough to make me close up my gloriously breezy open house.

Frigatebird

Frigatebird soars high
on seven foot wings shaped M,
scissor tail a V

Not So Wildlife

There is not much wildlife on St. Croix but what we have is fascinating. Most notable are three species of endangered sea turtles including the gigantic leatherback, iguanas that look like mini-dragons, a lizard that exists nowhere else in the world and sea birds with seven-foot wing spans.

There are no snakes, wild boar or poisonous spiders, not one really harmful creature.

Sea turtles nest on many tropical islands, but St. Croix seems to have an especially potent lure. Almost every beach is visited by at least one species every year, the Leatherback, Green and/or Hawksbill. Because the turtles are endangered, resident and visiting naturalists participate in formal or informal patrols to discourage poachers (who consider the eggs an aphrodisiac), relocate nests that are too close to the waterline, and escort hatchlings into the sea. Small, supervised groups of observers are allowed at the most active beaches. Both nesting and hatching take place after dark.

It is a thrilling privilege to watch a six-foot, 1,200-pound leatherback emerge from the sea, crawl up the beach, laboriously dig a two-foot hole in the sand with her huge back flippers, then hunker down to lay about 100 eggs. Most of the eggs look like cue balls but those on top are the size of ping pong balls and are sterile, apparently Nature's decoys to discourage digging predators. When she's finished laying, the leatherback fills the nest with sand and maneuvers around the area to camouflage the location of the nest, then returns to the water. The whole nesting process takes more than an hour.

Two months later that nest erupts with dozens of lively hatchlings, each the size of the palm of my hand.

Although each mother lays several nests throughout a season, the survival rate of the hatchlings is minuscule without human help. Their instinct is to head for light, which may take them inland. While traversing the beach they can be snatched by predators including birds, crabs and dogs. When they do enter the sea, they swim into the unknown immediately, without practice runs, without parental guidance or protection.

Beautiful Sandy Point National Wildlife Refuge on the west end of St. Croix is host to the largest known nesting aggregation of leatherbacks on U.S. territory. A research project underway there for several years hopes to determine the life-span of the leatherbacks (at least 50 years), the routes they travel (as far as Newfoundland), how often they return to nest (usually every two years between March and July) and if, as suspected, they nest on the beach where they were born. Computer chips implanted in each turtle enable tracking.

One established fact is that many sea turtles die after eating plastic bags they find floating in the ocean. The litter resembles jellyfish, their favorite food.

Earthwatch, an organization that provides volunteers for environmental and archeological projects internationally, supports the Sandy Point study with visitors who pay for the opportunity to walk the beach every night, spot the huge reptiles as they come ashore, and help the scientists collect their data.

Leatherbacks are an ancient species. Looking equally prehistoric are the Green Iguanas with their spiky dragon-like spines and long tails. They grow to six feet long overall and are fairly common on St. Thomas and St. John, less so on St. Croix. They are especially startling when young and a bright neon green. The first time I saw one disappearing into the bush I thought it was a plastic toy blown away from someone's pool. Mostly vegetarians with mild dispositions, they are sometimes raised as pets.

I have never laid eyes on the endangered reptile that lives only on two cays off the north coast of St. Croix— Protestant Cay, where there is a small resort, and Green Cay, a wildlife refuge that is off-limits to humans. The St. Croix Ground Lizard *(Ameiva polops)* is mostly brown and only a few inches long.

It looks similar to the ubiquitous *Anoli* lizard, a small gecko-like creature that enjoys human company. In open houses like mine the Anolis make themselves at home, scooting around quite harmlessly and hanging out patiently on the walls, resting on picture frames while waiting to pounce on passing mosquitoes and flies. Their coloring ranges from lime green to mahogany brown and, like chameleons, they change hue to blend with their surroundings. Households with cats do not welcome lizards, as a cat that eats a lizard can be sickened or even die.

We don't have any of the flashy bird species found elsewhere in the tropics—the brilliantly-colored parrots, macaws and toucans that lure bird-watchers from around the world. Our small population includes several endangered and threatened species and a number of migrants who, like the human "snowbirds" named after them, visit only in winter.

The most common and beloved of our native species is the small Yellow Breast, also known as Bananaquit or Sugarbird, the yellow bird of Harry Belafonte's calypso and the territorial bird of the Virgin Islands. They love sugar so much they will even eat from a human's hand.

Another personal favorite is the Cattle Egret or Tick Bird (locally called gaulin) which commutes past my house in a rippling white flock. At dawn they leave their roosts in nearby mangroves for fields where they spend the day eating insects, including ticks off the backs of grazing cows and horses. At dusk they flutter back past my gallery to the mangroves in the bay.

From my perch near the shoreline I also watch the spectacular Brown Pelican and Magnificent Frigatebird, both with wingspans up to seven feet. The pelican looks ungainly with its long beak and large pouch, but when it sights fish, it streamlines its silhouette and enters the water as straight as an Olympic diver. The frigate, black with white head and red throat, soars high in the thermal drafts, its angled wings creating a large M in the sky, its scissored tail a V. Lacking the protective oily feathers of most seabirds, it avoids the water by scooping up fish from the surface or, in an athletic feat also worthy of the Olympics, snatching prey already caught by other birds—in full flight.

Other St. Croix wildlife includes:

<u>White-tail Deer</u>, a pretty little creature which makes itself unpopular by trespassing on private land and, like the horses allowed to stray all over the island, eating prized vegetation. The deer were introduced by the French in the 1650s.

<u>Mongoose</u>: Our unofficial territorial mascot, this ferret-like carnivore was introduced to the islands in colonial times to devour snakes and rats in sugar cane fields. Rats, however, being nocturnal, escaped extinction by the diurnal mongooses. Despite their reputation as vicious, mongooses are kind of cute and some children have them as pets. One of my favorite books is "Up Mountain One Time" by Willie Wilson, a St. Thomas school teacher. It's a children's story about a lovable mongoose. (The accepted plural is mongooses, not mongeese. I like the Creole solution: mongoose dem.)

<u>Land crabs</u>, which are eaten whole or cut up in kallaloo. They live in mud near mangroves and emerge at night after a good rain. A road I often travel is prime hunting ground. I know the crabs are out and about if I encounter a car prowling slowly. When its headlights spot a crab, the car stops abruptly, all doors fly open and the entire family spews out, armed with flashlights, sticks, nets and buckets. Any traffic on the narrow and winding road must stop and wait as adults and children search the bushes by the side of the road for the elusive prey. Another indication of the laid-back goodwill that abounds here: I've never seen anyone object to this amusing delay.

<u>Whales and dolphin</u> are sighted offshore. Whales, particularly the acrobatic humpbacks, perform during the winter mating season. Dolphins frequently frolic near shore and I have friends who claim to have swum with them. I've never been so lucky but I have often met them when sailing. I love their permanent smiles and playful personalities. They seem to enjoy interacting with boats, particularly multihulls, diving under and leaping around the bows for several minutes at a time. When I was cruising, the arrival of dolphins was the most welcome diversion imaginable, especially on a long passage when the encounter could be our only living contact for days, even weeks.

Cattle

During the last half of the 20th Century, St. Croix was known in the cattle industry as the birthplace of the Senepol breed and its primary producer. Developed by local cattlemen by crossing the N'Dama from Senegal with the hornless Red Poll from England, the breed thrived in the hot, dry climate. Herds of handsome russet Senepols grazed on miles of rolling grasslands on the South Shore and animals were exported to many locations with similar weather, like Texas and Venezuela. Sadly, by 2001, most of the local herds were no longer profitable and were being sold off. The use of frozen semen was replacing the need for bulls, and ranchers also blamed high taxes, the high cost of air cargo and, weirdly, law suits by drivers whose vehicles collided with cows.

The island's creative farmers have also developed a breed of heat- and drought-resistant sheep. The animals are white and short-haired.

Island Mutts

Among the wild animals that roam the islands are many dogs and cats. The felines can rarely be tamed, but island canines make wonderful pets and guard dogs.

In St. Croix I've heard numerous terms to describe the local "breed": Heinz after the canned food company's 57 varieties, AKC (not American Kennel Club but All Kinds Crucian), Crucian Terriers, Crucian Shepherds, plain old Crucian Mutts and, my favorite, Coconut Retrievers. West Indians call them Funji Dogs.

There are of course pedigree fanciers who import Rottweilers, German Shepherds and other purebreds for companions and protectors, but for those of us who like mongrels, there is a perpetual supply of strays and "dumpster dogs," unwanted puppies dropped off with the garbage.

Multiple-dog households are common in the islands because there are so many strays that need homes, and the greater the number the better the security.

I have three island foundlings, one I adopted and two that adopted me.

My Number One dog in terms of age, acquisition and attachment is Benji. I found him at the animal shelter immediately after moving into my newly-built home. He was about six-months old, a smallish ball of white fluff, a shaggy-haired dog with floppy ears, big brown eyes and a little black button-nose—just the dog I had always wanted. I couldn't believe that someone had abandoned this darling pup and I could have him! He was the cutest thing I'd ever seen and, 15 years later, now deaf and half blind, he still makes my heart sing.

Benji and I were alone together for several years. We walked on the beach every morning. We exercised every afternoon—I swimming in the lap pool, he running back and forth on the side, occasionally falling in. We planted my garden together—we dug, I plugged, he dug.

Benji is a barker but not much of a protector. Such a cute little dog doesn't frighten many people. I knew I should have another, scarier animal on the property and one day Smiley showed up to take the job. I came home to find her—a typical Crucian Shepherd, a young female—reclining on the doormat outside my back door.

Amazingly, Benji accepted her. When I opened the door, expecting him to chase her away, he just stood there nonplussed as she walked in, allowing first a rambunctious investigation of his private parts and then a noisy attack on his food and water. We both watched politely as she made a quick but thorough house tour, then plopped down on the living room floor for a contented snooze. She had decided to stay.

Smiley loves to play, to run, jump and whirl after tennis balls or sticks, despite a limp from a broken leg in puppyhood. The parking area behind my house is her playground. A compulsive digger, she's turned the gravel driveway into a lunar landscape strewn with her toys—balls, bone shards, a mutilated flip-flop, a large suede shoe she carried up from the beach.

She is a born watchdog and she takes her job very seriously, barking at everything that comes within her range of sight, smell or hearing. She is really threatening to people who come up my driveway, and most West Indians won't get out of their cars or trucks until I remove her from their path.

I had no intention of acquiring a third dog when Bucky came into our lives, appearing on the beach, as strays often do. At first I thought he was a deer. He was skittish, had long spindly legs, huge upright ears, amber eyes and no tail that I could see because it was tucked so tightly between his legs. He craved human affection, and once he trusted me he nuzzled and snuggled at every opportunity. Naturally, I couldn't resist. Smiley was ecstatic to have a young playmate her own size. She and Bucky are almost a matched pair, both a beautiful shade of russet-brown with black muzzles.

I'm a hopeless disciplinarian but I'm not sure anyone could train Bucky. Domesticated, loving and lovable when it suits him, he is basically still a wild animal. If he suspects I want to curtail his freedom, by putting on a leash or shutting him in the house, he absolutely will not come to me, even if I have steak in my hand.

Still, he earns his keep performing hours of sentry duty on the stone wall in front of my house. Once he sounds the alert, all three dogs line up at attention and join in a barking chorus.

Their tails create a punctuation display. Benji's shaggy plumes are tightly curled in on themselves, like an ampersand. Smiley's feathery tail curves into a casual question mark. And Bucky, who seemed to have no tail when he was homeless and afraid, now carries his aloft—an exclamation point, I like to think, of joy.

@?!

Atmospheerie

Like a Japanese flag
the rising sun rests,
a flat red sphere on a wan white sky,
mysterious messenger of a windless day
when haze hangs murky over glassy sea
and distant islands, surprisingly clear and close,
hover like a mirage.
Fourteen hours later in the same frame of sky,
now a dull ghostly gray,
another red ball looms through the gloom—
the full moon cloaked in a pallid film,
a phantom of the night

Politics, Island Style

Many Americans who want to live on a tropical island deliberately choose an American possession because they feel secure under the benevolent protection of their own Uncle Sam. They don't have to worry about revolutions or *coups d'etats* as they would in a "banana republic," and there's no chance of being kicked out because they're foreigners. Their own flag and all it stands for, even filtered through left lane style, is reassuring.

The United States has many islands under its wing, mostly in the Pacific Ocean. Despite their far-flung locations, the island nations are administered, oddly enough, by the Department of the Interior.

In the Caribbean the U.S. possessions are Puerto Rico, a commonwealth, and the Virgin Islands, a territory. They have similar rights. Like states, they are governed by popularly-elected officials. Unlike states, they have no representation in the U.S. Congress except by one delegate, who can serve on committees but cannot vote on the floor. People born here are automatically U.S. citizens, but residents cannot vote for President.

The possessions do, however, benefit from Uncle Sam's voluminous pockets. In the V.I., although we pay federal income tax, the money does not go to Washington but stays in the territory. Millions more are given to the islands by the federal government every year to pump up basic services like schools, hospitals, welfare and roads.

Where the money goes is often a mystery, and allegations of "mismanagement" are common. Funds end up in the wrong department or agency, grants never reach the designated recipient and money earmarked for specific projects is never drawn. But millions still keep coming. Uncle Sam occasionally slaps our wrists and cuts back but he hasn't given up on us—yet.

On the local level, there is one territorial government for all of the U.S. Virgins, with the seat of government in St. Thomas. We elect a governor and lieutenant-governor every four years and 15 senators every two years. Proposals for changing the make-up and electoral base of the legislature are frequent, but as of 2001 we elect seven senators each from St. Thomas and St. Croix and one from St. John, who serves as a senator-at-large.

The territory has a huge deficit and is in fiscal crisis as we stumble into the 21st century. Not surprisingly, we have a problem finding willing candidates for the governor's hot-seat, where the buck stops. But everyone wants to be a V.I. senator. They are among the highest paid legislators in the country ($65,000 a year), have perks like chauffeur-driven cars, and are held accountable for very little. Some of them don't even consider it necessary to show up for meetings.

In the 2000 election there were 56 candidates vying for 15 seats. Voting machines were stressed to list them all, with nicknames. Aliases are such a part of V.I. culture they are routinely included in news stories, arrest reports, obituaries and even lists of senatorial candidates. Among our winners was Alicia "Chucky" Hansen and Donald "Ducks" Cole.

Almost all our public services are provided by the local government and most have a dismal reputation. Typically, the headlines play up what's wrong. The police have no working vehicles. Sewage flows into the sea. The roads are full of potholes. No one answers at 911. The landfill is burning. Litter covers the roadsides and beaches. The water is contaminated at one school and the toilets aren't working at another.

One crisis follows another. The government is broke and can't afford to fix the problems, but somehow we muddle through. The real wonder is that the services on these small isolated islands function as well as they do and that a breakdown is unusual enough to warrant media attention.

Financial distress is a convenient scapegoat but, miraculously, when any one predicament becomes critical (through a court order or a strike or a fine), our leaders pull a solution out of a hat by borrowing from another department, floating more bonds or mysteriously "finding" millions in some obscure fund.

Even if the territory were solvent, government left lane style would still be full of head-scratching, eyebrow-raising behavior. While we shake our heads in bewilderment over each new fiasco, we are not surprised. Eventually most of us even lose our sense of outrage. Outsiders, like the Crucians, learn to tolerate and even laugh at the debacle. And no matter how disastrous a situation becomes, most of us still have faith that if the local government really screws up, our reliable, indulgent Uncle Sam will come to the rescue.

The Dreaded DMV

The Department of Motor Vehicles in the V.I. has a notorious reputation. Most drivers have an incredulous tale to tell each time they visit the place.

To acquire or renew a license or registration, they can spend hours standing in line, often the wrong line due to a shortage of helpful signs, in the sun and in the rain. Frequently the wait is for naught. They finally reach the proper counter only to learn the camera isn't working, the computer is down, there aren't any license plates left, or it's simply closing time. Then they are told to come back again the next day.

While most West Indians appear to shrug and accept the situation, *que sera sera*, continentals frequently turn apoplectic over what they consider outrageous incompetence and indifference. But by the time they tell their latest story they're usually laughing too.

Getting an Education

Education has an unusual history in the U.S.V.I. Around 1840, when the colonial era was winding down, the progressive Danish governor, Peter von Scholten, made the unorthodox decision that all children in the Danish West Indies should go to school, including slaves.

He designed and built several handsome schoolhouses where the "unfree," as he called them, were taught by missionaries, members of the Moravian Brethren, an Eastern European sect that had settled on the island.

The missionaries had translated the Bible into English Creole, the common language of St. Croix despite the Danish administration. As they taught enslaved children to read the Bible, they nurtured the first generation of literate blacks.

The missionaries did not accept money for their school work, supporting themselves by trades, and they passed these skills along to their students as well, helping to prepare the "unfree" for emancipation when it came about, quite peacefully, in 1848.

Four of the St. Croix buildings known as the Von Scholten schools are still standing, though only one is still used as a school.

Today the territory's public education is provided as in the states. St. Croix has ten elementary schools, three junior high schools and two high schools.

Considering the small population and remoteness of the islands and the territorial government's failing grades in money management, the schools perform surprisingly well.

The media plays up the negatives such as violence among students and school buildings in dire need of repair, but those problems are generally restricted to a small percentage of the schools. Similarly, low teacher salaries and poor student scores in national tests are no worse than in comparable districts nationwide.

The reality is that the majority of the children who show up each day, spotlessly clean in their school uniforms, get an adequate education in a pleasant environment. Students motivated to acquire higher education often qualify for reputable colleges in the states and even win ample scholarships.

Many of the island's respected men and women are products of the V.I. public school system. The teachers who inspire them, including many continentals, are revered.

Students who choose to stay home for their higher education have a good but limited facility in the University of the Virgin Islands, which has campuses on St. Croix and St. Thomas. On St. Croix, the majority of the students are local residents with day jobs who attend classes in the evening.

Very few of the continentals in the U.S.V.I. send their children to public schools. Unlike many remote outposts, the territory has several good private schools and most children stay on-island for their education, at least through high school.

St. Croix has four schools, including a Catholic one, that span the years from kindergarten through twelfth grade. Most of their graduates get into good colleges in the states. There are also many smaller private schools including Montessori classes for young children and a number of church-affiliated academies. Home-schooling is fairly popular.

There was one Arcadian private school in the late 60s and early 70s that teachers and students still talk about with great fondness. Tamarind was created by a group of progressive teachers who built their own open-air "classrooms" within the ruins of an old plantation in "the bush." Theirs was a hands-on approach to education, with science classes snorkeling off the beach or walking forest trails to study the animals and plants they found there and literature classes acting out plays on stages they constructed in the trees.

Children who grow up in the Virgin Islands and attend private schools here acquire one priceless asset their counterparts on the mainland rarely enjoy. Mingling naturally with playmates and schoolmates of all races and ethnic backgrounds they are hardly aware of differences. They are blissfully "colorblind." If they leave this Garden of Eden for the "real world," the most surprising and distressing loss of innocence is discovering that in America racial prejudice still exists.

Famous Furniture

St. Croix is famous in antiques circles for its West Indian plantation-era furniture made by local craftsmen. Most sought after are four-poster beds and planter's chairs, the low-slung seats on whose extended arms a planter rested his legs until swelling subsided enough for a slave or servant to pull off his boots.

The island's distinctive style was modeled on European classics and adapted to beautiful local hardwoods, especially Swietenia, a West Indies Mahogany, that could withstand the tropical climate and wood-boring insects.

Whim Museum showcases locally-made furnishings, and a leading stateside furniture manufacturer has copied pieces in the Whim collection for a very popular line of West Indian reproductions.

Whim also holds an annual antiques auction that fetches high prices from far-flung buyers, but some of the old families on the island aren't yet aware that their old furnishings are valuable. It's still fairly common to come across broken pieces discarded in a dumpster.

Speaking the Language

West Indians speak a Creole language, dialect or patois, a mix of European and African words distilled through the Caribbean experience. The word connotes a melding of the new world with the old and can allude to the people, their food and pastimes as well as the language they speak.

On French or Dutch islands the Creole is recognizably French or Dutch. On British and American islands an English-Creole is spoken. In the V.I., although the language is basically English, there is so much Creole in the speed, usage, odd inflections and expressions that there are times when English-speaking non-West Indians can hardly understand it.

Well-educated Virgin Islanders are bilingual, sliding easily from Creole to standard English depending on the people present. There is a slight difference between the dialects of the three main U.S. Virgins: Thomian, Johnian and Crucian.

I love the simplicity of this unwritten language. There aren't any "rules," but here are some generalizations:

Personal pronouns are unpredictable: Me talk Crucian. I does eat. He marry she.

Tenses are expressed indirectly: I does work. Me done eat. I been there (yesterday). I gon see you (tomorrow).

Words are repeated for emphasis: bad-bad, far-far.

A couple of pronunciation quirks:

Words are sometimes accented on the "wrong" syllable: recog<u>nize</u>, sophisti<u>ca</u>ted.

Th is pronounced as d or t: ting for thing, duh for the, dem for them and wid for with.

Here is a brief "dictionary" of some commonly used Crucian or V.I. terms, spelled as they sound.

all mash up = broken

anti-man = homosexual

ax = ask

bahn ya = born here

beforetime = formerly

bush = brush, wilderness

bush medicine = medicine made from a plant

bush tea = tea made from a plant; herbal tea

bush woman = woman who knows medicinal uses of herbs and plants

dem = them, often connoting plural as in duh people dem

fadda = father

finish = finished, out of

flim = film

for true = really

gone bush = disappeared

gut = gully, stream, small river

jeese an bread! = exclamation like for goodness sake, gosh

jumbie = spirit

kwart = quarter, 25 cent piece

limin = hanging out, talking

make 35 = have 35th birthday

makin a baby = pregnant

melée = gossip or rumor (rarely the standard meaning of ruckus or fracas)

mocko jumbie = stilt dancer dressed like a jumbie

mudda = mother

next = another, more

onliest = only

outside chile = child by a man or woman who is not a husband or wife

pistarkle = melée

presha = high blood pressure

Rasta box = boom box, radio

reach = arrive

rum shop = downscale bar

shugah = diabetes

ting = thing; often used like etcetera as in rain, wind and ting.

upstairs house = two-story house

walk with = carry, take

Spanglish

With the large Hispanic population on St. Croix, we hear a lot of "Spanglish," a charming mix of Spanish and English languages. Those who are bilingual switch effortlessly back and forth between the two languages, often several times in one sentence. Even Hispanics who don't speak English fluently sprinkle their conversations with American terms. Here are just a few samples:

tomar un break = to take a break
pagar con cash = to pay with cash
trabajo overtime = overtime work
Me voy shopping = I'm going shopping

Gardening in Eden

Tropical vegetation is exuberant and flashy, with showy flowers and shapely foliage flourishing irrepressibly year around. It's so easy to grow things in the islands ornamental gardening is a joy, and anyone with a bit of ground or even a few pots becomes an enthusiastic gardener.

When I settled on St. Croix I learned everything I needed to know about planting my own tropical garden by volunteering in the nursery at St. George Village Botanical Garden. This is where the island's avid gardeners have created a world-class tourist attraction and educational site and where I became acquainted with the local custom of sharing gardening material. My original "landscaping" was a hodge-podge of hand-me-downs given to me as seeds, cuttings, seedlings or full-grown plants. I stuck them all in the ground and most of them flourished, just as beautiful as the more planned garden that has evolved.

The frequent showers and daily warm sunshine of the tropics are ideal conditions for growing. On the high islands where precipitation is significant, houses are dwarfed by their surrounding vegetation. Even on dry St. Croix, a large percentage of gardening time is spent cutting back the "jungle." Here is a telling statistic: In the V.I. 40 percent of landfill material is yard scraps. And that's despite the expanding use of home composting.

Jungle is an appropriate metaphor because danger lurks in the lush growth. Sometimes it seems the more beautiful the plant the more lethal its defenses. Many species including the ebullient bougainvillea have nasty thorns. A few such as poinsettia and oleander have poisonous sap. Gardeners must handle them carefully and plant them only where animals and children can't be harmed.

The variety of tropical vegetation is overwhelming and landscaping has infinite possibilities. Want palm trees? There are 1,500 species to choose from. Love flowering shrubs? There are hundreds. Crave blossoms every day? Bougainvillea and hibiscus, those gorgeous symbols of the tropics, oblige—in many different colors.

In most places it seems the lusty plants will flourish no matter what, but there are areas where growing anything is a struggle.

In some locations on St. Croix there is a soil that's actually white, called caliche. The only way to grow anything in it is to dig big holes and fill them with topsoil. And there are areas that are so windswept and/or blasted by salt from the sea that very little survives. But the determined gardener can always find something to adorn his grounds. Even on the beaches there are sea grapes, mahoes, coconut palms and cacti.

The only adversaries that can really defeat a serious grower are insects, which also thrive here. I have given up trying to grow vegetables. Their predators are so ravenous an entire crop can disappear overnight. The ornamental plants are tougher, usually able to recover from an onslaught of mealybugs, aphids, scale, whitefly, caterpillars or worms.

One notable exception was a plague of pink mealybugs that attacked hibiscus and some vegetable crops throughout the territory in the late 1990s. Hibiscus is probably the most popular plant in the tropics. It is easy to grow, produces flowers in many stunning colors and shapes, blooms almost every day (though each blossom lasts only one or two days) and can be grafted and hybridized quite readily.

When the pink mealybug struck, it was a territorial disaster. The Department of Agriculture imported natural predators, tiny wasps, and released them throughout the islands. Some desperate gardeners invested $70 an ounce in a chemical that seemed effective. Even so, many of us lost all our hibiscus.

I rarely find anything to admire about garden pests but the hornworm that gobbles the leaves of frangipani trees is a beauty worth mentioning. Like a giant caterpillar, it's up to six inches long and half an inch around, black with horizontal yellow stripes, a red head and an orange "horn" on its rear end. It is so spectacular I wouldn't dream of harming it.

For the environment's sake I resist most chemical spraying. When I have pests I usually let nature take its course or I cut off affected areas or I spray with a home remedy called SOS. That's four teaspoons baking Soda, four teaspoons cooking Oil and two teaspoons dishwashing Soap to one gallon of water, applied after sunset so the hot sun doesn't "cook" the oil on the foliage. If a plant dies despite my ministrations I figure it didn't belong in my garden and I replace it with something else.

A logical solution to growing problems, and that promoted by organizations involved with trees and shrubs, is to plant only native species, which are resistant to local pests and hardy enough to withstand local conditions, from droughts to hurricanes. But sadly the native species rarely measure up visually to exotic imported species and most gardeners, including me, continue to take their chances with beautiful aliens.

There are reference books galore full of glorious pictures and information about tropical plants. This list covers only a few of special interest to me, if only because of a fetching local name.

TREES

<u>Frangipani</u>—Oriental shape, lovely sweet-smelling flowers.

<u>Poor Man's Orchid</u>—the blossoms resemble orchids.

<u>Flamboyant</u>—Aptly named, it looks like a giant scarlet umbrella from May to November. It belongs to the Poinciana family, named after Phillippe de Poincy, a 17th century governor of the French West Indies, which briefly included St. Croix.

<u>Turpentine Tree</u>—locally known as Tourist Tree because it's red and peeling.

<u>Manchineel</u> (or Manganeel)—The entire tree is poisonous, from the bark to small apple-like fruit. Even rain dripping from the tree can blister skin.

<u>Thibet</u>—known as Woman Tongue or Mother-in-law Tongue because of clacking pods. (Sanseveria, a succulent ground cover, is also called Mother-in-law Tongue. Its leaves are long and sharp.)

<u>Mangrove</u>—Ecologically crucial, forests of these small trees grow in wetlands, where they protect the land from

103

storm surge and the sea from runoff. Their aerial roots are nurseries for marine life.

Baobab—a massive tree with a long lifespan, spiritually important in its native Africa. Enslaved Africans brought seeds to the Caribbean, hidden between their teeth according to one story.

Lignum Vitae—"Tree of Life." Its "ironwood" was used on old ships.

Ginger Thomas or Yellow Cedar or Yellow Elder—its trumpet-shaped blossoms are the territorial flower.

Shower of Gold—as beautiful as it sounds.

Calabash—produces round gourds that make wonderful musical instruments and bowls.

MISCELLANEOUS

Guinea Grass—a tall grass that grows wild all over the islands.

Cut Leaf Philodendron—two-foot leaves are deeply indented, a Jolly Green Giant.

Swiss Cheese—a philodendron with holes.

Firecracker—a shrub with spectacular sprays of bright red tubes that do indeed look like firecrackers.

Lady of the Night—a flowering shrub that smells like cheap perfume.

Mexican Creeper—a vine that beautifies fences and derelict buildings with gorgeous sprays of fuchsia flowers.

Poinsettia—an expansive shrub that sometimes grows to tree size, the very same plant so popular in small pots in northern climes at Christmas time, when its leaves turn red.

Tan-Tan—an undesirable, irrepressible scrubby tree with fern-like foliage and long tap root.

<u>Century Plant</u>—an uninteresting agave until age seven (not 100), when it sprouts a central shoot several feet tall, like a giant asparagus stalk, with big round clusters of golden flowers, then dies.

<u>Night-Blooming Cereus</u>—an ugly creepy cactus with magnificent flowers that bloom just one night. White petals open like a huge scalloped chalice brimming with silky yellow threads.

Flamboyant

Flamboyant tree so
aptly named pops umbrella
of scarlet flowers

Precious Water

Fresh water is so precious in the Virgin Islands we call it liquid gold. Unlike many of the islands, which have high mountains attracting heavy rainfall, the Virgins have relatively low mountains and little rain. St. Croix is particularly dry because it is flatter and has fewer trees, the result of clearing for cultivation in the plantation era. Water or the lack of it is our number one topic of conversation.

In the 15 years I've lived on St. Croix there has been no such thing as a "rainy season." May and November are historically the wettest months, but often those months are arid too.

Since piped "town" water is not available everywhere, buildings are required to include cisterns for storing water, with a capacity of at least 10 gallons per square foot of roof. Cisterns are usually large concrete holding tanks, often divided into two or more chambers, built under the foundation instead of a basement. They collect rainwater from the roof. There's no music more beautiful than the gurgle and splash of rainwater traveling down spouts into cisterns. A cistern pump automatically delivers water when a faucet or tap is turned on.

Some hotels and private homes have sweet-water wells and/or their own desalination plants to augment rainfall.

Those who don't must buy water when it doesn't rain. We have a choice of well water, which is cheap but often brackish, or desalinated water, distilled by the local Water and Power Authority (WAPA).

The water is delivered by private water trucks and pumped into the cistern through large hoses inserted in an overflow pipe. To keep out frogs, leaves and other foreign bodies, overflow pipes and downspouts are screened.

There are several sizes of water trucks on St. Croix that carry between 2,700 gallons and 10,000 gallons. In 2001 well water cost about 3.5 cents a gallon and distilled water about 4.5 cents. I buy 3,600 gallons at a time for $165.

Cistern water from WAPA or the rain god is usually considered drinkable, but periodic chlorinating is recommended to kill any bacteria that might be washed down from the roof, and most people use filters to remove sediment and other undesirable properties.

Because our water is so precious, we are very stingy about it, conserving every possible drop and scolding guests who blithely let the water run while brushing teeth or washing dishes. We make everyone take Navy showers, running the water only to get wet and rinse off, and we recycle shower, laundry and dishwater, soap and all, to keep our plants alive.

Called "gray water," it is collected in anything from buckets to elaborate plumbed tanks or is channeled directly to a particular area. My washing machine empties into a flower bed where I've cultivated a luxuriant stand of papyrus, a plant that likes water better than soil. It is the most successful thing in my garden.

Toilets that use minimal water are naturally popular here, and the local energy office promotes their purchase by offering rebates on them. Still, many of us flush only when necessary, a rather gross custom we try to lighten with humor as in these couplets posted in many public lavatories:

> *In these isles of sun and fun*
> *We never flush for Number One.*

Or,

> *If it's yellow let it mellow,*
> *If it's brown flush it down.*

Composting toilets and private sewage-treatment plants are just starting to catch on in the V.I. I predict they will become very popular when homeowners and resort developers realize how green and lush their grounds can be from the "black" water created by treating and recycling human waste.

Clever islanders have known this all along. They always plant their banana trees on the septic tank drain field, often a green oasis on otherwise brown ground.

Fire

Brush fires are frequent on this dry island where acres of undeveloped land are covered with wild grasses, sometimes tall as a man. A smoldering cigarette, a glass bottle ignited by the hot sun, or an arsonist starts a fire and the tradewinds turn it into a galloping inferno of leaping flames that consume miles within minutes.

Luckily, we have a good fire service. Like all government departments it operates under budgetary duress, is poorly equipped and under-staffed (with only government employees, no volunteers). Nevertheless, it does a good job.

With fire hydrants only in and around the towns, the only source of water in the fields is whatever is in the tanker. The fire fighters let the brush burn, wisely saving water until they really need it—when the flames near something valuable, like a house or animal corral.

Brush Fire

In the smoky night after the fire engines have gone
the field still writhes with smoldering brush
and glowing embers that once were trees—
red stick figures, loose-jointed, skeletal,
death-dance on the blackened wasteland,
detonating as they self-destruct.

Island Cuisine

West Indians eat heartily. Their "plate of food" at any time of day will likely be heaped high with meat, chicken or fish, some kind of rice dish and starchy vegetables.

In the U.S.V.I., anyone who prefers a different diet is in luck, as grocery stores now carry most of the same products as stateside stores and many restaurants cater to stateside tastes.

St. Croix is graced with so many good restaurants, dining out is a major form of recreation. There are several gourmet restaurants to choose from as well as a cross-section of ethnic eateries and some that specialize in vegetarian fare. Many of the American fast-food chains are represented here too and, of course, numerous restaurants, "cook shops" and mobile vans serving "local" cuisine.

There are many good books devoted to Virgin Islands or Caribbean cuisine. As a non-cook, I have nothing to add but observations.

<u>Starchy vegetables and grains</u>: Coming from a tradition of hardship and poverty, West Indians have learned to satisfy their hunger with starchy, filling foods. There are several varieties of root vegetables, called ground provisions. Their names differ on different islands and include sweet potato, tania, casava, kava, taro and yam. Rice is a staple at almost every meal: rice and beans, rice and

(pigeon) peas, fry rice or season rice (as we say in Creole). Baked macaroni and cheese is a favorite side dish, as are plantains (that look and taste like bananas but must be cooked) and potato stuffing (mashed white potatoes mixed with tomato sauce, milk, eggs, raisins and seasonings, then baked). Fungi, a stiff cornmeal mush, sometimes with okra added, is usually paired with fish.

<u>Green vegetables</u> are not prized. A major exception is kallaloo (or callaloo), a gumbo-like dish based on leaves from the kallaloo bush. Crabmeat is a desirable addition to this dish.

<u>Meat</u>: The star attraction at important occasions is often a whole animal—pig or goat—roasted on a spit over an open fire. Meat is also part of most daily diets. Once an animal is killed, nothing is wasted. Odd animal parts are featured in several popular dishes such as bull foot soup; souse, a stew based on pig's head or feet; and goat water, soup from a goat head.

<u>Fast food, Caribbean style</u>: Meat, chicken (including the bones), seafood or vegetables are wrapped to go, either as roti, a tortilla-like cake of flour and water around a curried filling; or as patés or patties, filled pastry shells. Roti is an East Indian dish via Trinidad.

<u>Fish</u> is naturally a major part of the diet. Grouper and snapper are probably the most populous and popular foods from the sea, even though snapper can carry ciguatera, a serious fish poisoning. Restaurants snap up most of the desirable deep-water fish (tuna, wahoo and dolphin—not the porpoise relative but a smaller fish also known as *mahi-mahi* in Polynesian or *dorado* in Spanish). Small reef fish or "potfish" (they are often caught in traps or "pots" and they

are usually boiled in pots) come in many species, including the queen trigger, locally known as old wife. Oddly, despite the other choices available today—fresh, frozen, canned—many West Indians still buy saltfish, cod or herring that has been salted and dried.

<u>Shellfish</u>: The Caribbean lobster, or *langousta*, is clawless, closer to the South African rock lobster than the Maine lobster. Most plentiful is spiny lobster. Two smaller kinds that are especially succulent are the slipper lobster that looks like an armored tank and the margarita that resembles a giant shrimp. Conch, the slimy creature that lives in the big beautiful shell, is very tough, but when tenderized by pounding or pressure cooking is popular in fritters, chowder, stew, roti and patés. Whelk, a large snail in a black and white shell, is a similar, more tender, food. Land crabs are purged with cornmeal for three days, then cooked and served whole or cut up in kallaloo. Marine crabs are now rare. Bivalves are just about extinct.

<u>Tropical fruits</u> are heavenly. Almost-too-good-to-be-true are succulent mangos, melon-like papayas, tangy Key limes and the smallest, sweetest bananas imaginable, called bakobas. There are also guavas, genips, pineapples, soursop, oranges, grapefruit, passion fruit and 17 kinds of "apples," none of which resemble those that grow in northern countries. The island "pear" is avocado.

<u>Sweets</u>: Local cakes and tarts, puddings and candy tend to be <u>very</u> sweet.

<u>Snack:</u> Johnny Cake is deep-fried dough—the islands' donut, without the hole. It is served as a side dish or snack and is a local food that non-adventurous outsiders can readily enjoy.

Soft Drinks: Interesting, healthy drinks made from local plants include gingerbeer, passion fruit juice, sea moss (from seaweed), sorrel (a Christmas drink made from sorrel blossoms) and hibiscus (from the lovely flowers). Maubi (from the bark of the mauby tree) is a non-alcoholic beer.

Hard Drinks: The one true bargain in the duty-free Virgin Islands is liquor. There is no tax on any alcoholic beverage and, except for election day, there is never a problem acquiring something to drink. Booze flows where water is strictly rationed. Shops of all kinds sell it and there are bars or "rum shops" on every corner.

Rum is the spirit of choice throughout the Caribbean, dating back to colonial days and the pervasive sugar cane plantations. Rum is made from molasses, which is a by-product of sugar, and most sugar plantations produced rum. An excellent brand, Cruzan Rum, is still made on St. Croix but, ironically, since sugar isn't grown here anymore, the molasses for the rum has to be shipped in from other places. Still rum is cheaper than the soft drinks it's mixed with, and bartenders pour accordingly.

Alcohol consumption decreased dramatically here as elsewhere in the 1990s, and water bottles have replaced a good many of the ubiquitous beer bottles. But the islands continue to have a more than average share of people with drinking problems, and Alcoholics Anonymous is active. Those who succeed in sobering up here are doubly proud, that they were able to do it, and do it *here*.

115

Frangipani

Sweet frangipani
perfumes island gardens from
Chinese brushstroke limbs

Spiritual Life

People in St. Croix practice a fascinating mix of "civilized" and "primitive" beliefs. As in other cultures where missionaries have trod, the natives, or in this case enslaved Africans, politely accepted what the missionaries taught them, then quietly incorporated old beliefs into the new. It's not unusual to find devout Christians who believe in "jumbies," spirits from the African heritage, or even witchcraft. Forms of sorcery such as voodoo, obeah or santeria, which are usually linked with other Caribbean islands, especially Haiti, can also be found here but their practice is very hush-hush.

St. Croix is famous for its many churches, about 150 at last count, more per capita than anywhere else in the U.S.A. I read somewhere. That's one for every 350 people and one per every square half-mile.

A directory published by the island's Interfaith Coalition in 1999 includes houses of worship for these faiths, among others: AME (African Methodist Episcopalian), Anglican or Episcopal, Baha'i, Baptist (11), Buddhist, Church of Jesus Christ of Latter-Day Saints (Mormon), Islamic, Jehovah's Witnesses, Jewish, Lutheran, Methodist, Pentecostal (19 of them, 16 Spanish-speaking), Roman Catholic, Seventh Day Adventist (8) and Unitarian Universalist. It did not include all the groups that meet in living rooms or storefronts or the frequent evangelical revival meetings held under huge tents.

Religion is central in the lives of many of the residents here, a fact credited for a population of unusually kind and caring people and a general aura of spirituality. Religious tolerance is part of the tradition. Even the Jews and Arabs get along here. While the Muslims were building their mosque, they held their services next door in the Jewish synagogue.

Two unusual religions with many followers here are Moravian and Rastafarian.

Lutheran was Denmark's state religion during the colonial era (and still is) but the Danes, in desperate need of settlers for their West Indian colony, welcomed people of all faiths.

Starting in 1732, missionaries from the Moravian sect in eastern Europe came, to convert slaves to Christianity and later to teach slave children. There are still three Moravian churches on the island: Friedensthal (Peaceful Valley) in Christiansted, Friedensfeld (Peaceful Field) mid-island and Friedensberg (Peaceful Hill) in Frederiksted.

Rastafarianism, a religion indigenous to the Caribbean, worships a black messiah. It originated in Jamaica in the early 20th century when Marcus Garvey led a nationalistic Back to Africa movement among descendants of former slaves. He prophesied the crowning of an African King of Kings. In 1930, when Ras Tafari Makonnen was crowned Emperor Haile Selassie of Ethiopia, Garvey proclaimed the emperor the messiah of the black man.

Selassie was descended from an Abyssinian line reaching back to King Solomon and the Queen of Sheba. He died in 1975 but, like Jesus, he is thought to transcend mortality.

Rastafarians (Rastas for short) call their god Jah. They are best known for wearing their hair in locks (or "dreadlocks"); their use of marijuana, smoked to encourage religious meditation (though some groups frown on that); and for reggae, the music that is associated with the religious movement. The late Bob Marley, a reggae superstar, helped make Rastafarianism international.

An odd footnote: The British Virgin Islands for many years enforced a law designed expressly to keep out Rastafarians and "hippies" by prohibiting dreadlocks and other long hair styles. They finally repealed the act in 1999.

Living Cathedral

My church is a drive-through,
a stretch of rainforest road
where soaring mahoganies vault across the sky.

The leafy sanctuary
is hushed and shady,
cool and damp.

My little red Honda slows to a reverent crawl.

I worship trees that rose from hurricane-dead,
small birds that sing divinely,
and dappled sunlight blessing the lane.

I receive absolution from a sudden tropical shower.

I am renewed when I come out the other side.

A Healing Environment

The Caribbean is a healing environment. People who arrive with aches and pains or chronic diseases often feel amazingly better after a few days of warm sunshine, soft breezes, therapeutic salt water and the slow pace of island life. It sounds like the perfect place to spend one's golden years, right?

Yes, if you don't get a serious illness.

Many of the continentals who live here are retirees looking forward to enjoying their final years in paradise. All too often their idyll ends when they develop a medical condition that can't be treated here and they feel they must move back to the mainland for health care. Hopefully the exodus will stop soon, if V.I. hospitals achieve their goal of health care equal to stateside standards.

St. Croix has the potential to become medically self-sufficient. Many good doctors practice here, including a rapidly increasing number of specialists, and in 2001 the Juan Luis Hospital passed the Joint Commission on the Accreditation of Healthcare Organizations for the third consecutive time. It is the only hospital in the Eastern Caribbean with that all-important accreditation.

The picture should keep getting better. The territory's two hospitals, Juan Luis and the Roy Schneider Hospital in St. Thomas, made a big leap forward in 2000 by shedding some government control. They became semi-autonomous, taking over management of their own finances, procurement and staff, and immediately started turning around their reputations. Even continentals used to the highest medical standards reported good experiences at the hospitals. And many outpatient services, like CT scans and colonoscopies, for which patients formerly had to go off-island, are now available at home.

Previously, under the total control of the financially-challenged territorial government, the hospitals struggled with antiquated medical equipment, few specialists and a chronic shortage of nursing staff, medicines and supplies. Patients frequently had to bring their own linens and, West Indian style, rely on family members to empty bed pans and bring food. A stay in a local hospital was dreaded, and many potential patients invested in air ambulance insurance to make sure they could get out if they needed hospital care.

It now seems realistic to hope that all our health care needs can someday be met on the island.

Here is a dream for St. Croix, which needs a new source of income and still has plenty of undeveloped land: a complete medical complex including a full-service hospital; convalescent, rehabilitation and nursing home facilities; and links to the many alternative/complementary healing arts practiced here such as yoga, massage, acupuncture, meditation, homeopathic, chiropractic and herbal.

Residents would not have to go off-island for treatment and non-residents from the Caribbean, the states, the world, would come here for medical attention and to enjoy the healing environment. The island would become a desirable health care/retirement destination and the territory would profit.

The government, apparently unwilling to lose control, has so far been unreceptive to proposals for such facilities from the private sector. Leon Hess of Hess Oil, after opening a huge refinery on St. Croix in the 1960s, offered to give a complete hospital to the island and was turned down. We can only pray the attitude will change some day.

Bush Medicine

With the world-wide rekindling of interest in herbal and other natural remedies, the weed women of the Caribbean have re-emerged as acceptable healers. In colonial days, slaves who knew the medicinal properties of plants provided the only medical care for fellow Africans, and they sometimes treated the white people too. They were highly respected, as their knowledge had to include not just which plant cured what ailment but which part of the plant, what time of year to harvest it, how to prepare it and, above all, how to avoid any toxic properties. Modern weed women have to know all that as well as the dangers of combining natural remedies with manufactured drugs.

Plant remedies are believed to cure everything from colds and upset stomachs to leukemia, tuberculosis and venereal diseases. They are administered as poultices, baths, infusions or teas. Bush teas (made from leaves, grasses, flowers, roots or bark) are the most common treatments. Often the same tea is prescribed for a number of apparently unrelated problems: Castor Bean leaf tea treats stomach ache and fever; Vetiver root tea is drunk for flu, fever, pleurisy and yellow fever; and the leaf of Whitehead Broom is used in a tea for colds, heart troubles and stomach ache.

Fun and Games

What is there to *do* there, acquaintances in the states often ask, as if living in paradise must get boring after a while.

People who must have shopping malls or concert halls obviously won't be happy here. But for most of those who choose to live on a tropical island it's a fair assumption that the lack of such amenities is one of the pluses. They're looking for natural surroundings and more simple, laid-back pleasures to fill their leisure time.

I stopped working in 1994 and have been so busy ever since I wonder how I ever had time to fit in a job. Among the activities I attend weekly are a writers' workshop and a weekly gathering of artists who meet to paint in a different location each time. These happen to be groups I started with one or two friends. They have both taken on a life of their own.

There are many other pastimes to choose from. Here are some of particular interest to continentals on St. Croix. Clubs come and go, of course, but I include those I know are operating in 2001.

WATER SPORTS

<u>Swimming and snorkeling</u>: There are numerous beaches with excellent swimming in the warm, enticing Caribbean

Sea. Many of them are good for snorkeling as well, with coral close to shore. Oddly, many West Indians never learn to swim, but continental kids who grow up here often become champion swimmers. There are two large swim teams for school children. Long-distance swimmers get together regularly, and there is an annual five-mile coral reef swim race that brings in international competitors.

Surfing: There is a small corps of enthusiasts but the surf is rarely up.

Wind-surfing: The tradewinds, steady and often strong, make conditions ideal.

Scuba diving: Diving sites here are among the best in the Caribbean. They include the famous Wall, a steep coral drop-off paralleling the north shore.

BOATING

Sailing: Unlike the other Virgins, both American and British, St. Croix does not offer endless island-hopping opportunities. The only off-shore destination is Buck Island, but both snorkeling and beaching are so good there many boaters happily return every weekend. Despite the lack of places to go nearby, there are many sailboats filling a few good anchorages, three marinas and an active yacht club that promotes several races yearly.

Kayaking: Paddlers are close to nature in protected bays and often calm coastal waters.

Sport fishing: There are several boats for hire and a few tournaments every year.

LAND SPORTS

<u>Golf</u>: There are two beautiful 18-hole golf courses, one designed by Robert Trent Jones, and there is one 9-hole course.

<u>Tennis</u>: There are many courts available to residents, in public parks and at hotels. There is one private tennis club.

<u>Running</u>: A race club holds frequent events. A number of residents participate in the island's biggest sporting event of the year, a triathlon that attracts athletes from around the world. In 2001 it became a qualifying race for the Ironman in Hawaii and drew over 800 competitors. The famous "Beast" on the biking segment of the race is a 600-foot hill with a .7 mile climb at grades up to 18%.

<u>Biking</u>: There is a racing bike club and a mountain bike club.

<u>Hiking</u>: A hiking club often designs its routes to take in sites of historical and/or ecological interest, sometimes adding lectures or poetry readings along the way.

<u>Horseback Riding</u>: Pony clubs for kids are active. A couple of stables provide guided riding tours.

<u>Horse Racing</u>: About once a month there are horse races with pari-mutuel betting.

TEAM SPORTS: Croquet and cricket are played here, as well as baseball, basketball, soccer, football, bowling and darts.

TABLE GAMES: Several bridge groups meet regularly. There are scrabble and chess clubs. Weekly games of Trivial Pursuit are held at various locations.

GYMS: There are a few gyms and one comprehensive health and fitness club with pool.

GARDENING: Both experts and novices are welcome as volunteers at the St. George Village Botanical Garden. There are hibiscus, fern, orchid and bonsai societies.

ARTS

Painting: The island has many excellent artists, including many outsiders drawn here by the local beauty, color and light. There are several galleries, a few large group shows annually, and frequent classes, workshops and arts and crafts fairs.

Dancing: There are a couple of ballet schools and one of Caribbean dance, which provides continuous talent for a company that performs world-wide.

PRIVATE CLUBS: A tennis club, a yacht club, a beach club and some just plain social clubs have almost exclusively continental members.

SPECIAL INTEREST GROUPS: People with a common interest often form informal groups that meet on a more or less regular basis. Writers, photographers, *plein-air* artists, quilters, book readers and ham radio operators are among them.

ENTERTAINMENT

Music: An annual series of candlelight concerts in the 18th century greathouse of Whim Museum brings in chamber music ensembles from around the world. Island Center, a large amphitheater, usually schedules several concerts a year, from classical to rock and gospel (although as I write in 2001, the wonderful facility is broke and barely functioning). Night clubs and restaurant/bars have a steady diet of imported and local talent. On almost any night some kind of music can be heard, soft piano or cool jazz for dining, island music or the latest stateside craze for dancing. In a good year there might be an international festival of jazz, blues or Caribbean music.

<u>Theater</u>: A community theater presents several plays a year. Other groups stage occasional shows.

<u>Film</u>: Eight small movie theaters show first-run films. Occasionally foreign films are shown by private organizations.

<u>Poetry</u>: Poetry readings are held often, sometimes in conjunction with music, dance or fine art.

<u>Fairs</u>: An annual agricultural fair is one of the most popular events of the year. Street fairs featuring bands, mocko jumbies, food and drink, and arts and crafts are frequent in both towns. They're called Jump Ups in Christiansted and Harbour Nights in Frederiksted.

Emy Thomas

Dappled Sunlight

*Dappled sunlight dots
forest road with dancing blips
of shadow and shine*

Is It Safe?

Like most places in the world today, paradise has crime. The Caribbean, conveniently located between drug-producing South America and drug-buying North America, is a natural conduit for the illegal trade and the American islands, with their ready access to the U.S.A., are quite active.

Tragically, a lot of the contraband remains in the islands, with a relatively low street price, creating a vigorous drug trade on the local level and an abundance of drug-related crimes.

The U.S. Virgin Islands ranks poorly in national statistics. On a per capita basis it has one of the highest rates of murder, rape and robbery in the country. The good news is that the homicide rate has dropped dramatically. There were 18 murders in the territory in 2000 compared to 35 in 1998. The bad news is that the islands still had twice the national average, 13.3 (compared to 6) per 100,000 residents.

Despite the frightening statistics, continentals are reasonably safe, as outsiders are not often the victims of violent crimes. Unlike some places in the Caribbean where white people have been definitely targeted, Virgin Islands criminals tend to prey on their own. Most of the murders are by young black men who kill other young black men in drug deals gone wrong. Most of the rapes are by West Indian men violating females they know well, all too often children.

Theft (or teefing as we say in Crucian) is more sweeping. Most incidents are considered drug-motivated, with users stealing to finance their habits. Apparently they select their victims quite randomly, without regard to race, age, sex or even apparent affluence. The police blotter lists a surprising number of thefts in public housing areas in addition to businesses, homes and people on the street and, shockingly, churches and schools.

Many of the crimes are never solved or prosecuted, a failure usually blamed on the government's chronic financial crisis. There is simply not enough money to fund an adequate police force with sufficient equipment or maintenance thereof.

On St. Croix it seems that at least once a year there are a few days with no police cars on the road and officers have to walk, take a bus or hitchhike to the scene of a crime. It sounds like a joke, but isn't.

Neither is the adage about knowing the right people. The low rate of arrests and convictions is due partly to under-funding of Public Safety and Justice Departments and partly to conflicts of interest within a small community. The perpetrator has a good chance of being related to someone in the system, and he often remains free.

Unfortunately, information about crime in the Virgin Islands would be incomplete without mention of the Fountain Valley "massacre." This is the incident that abruptly changed the image and direction of St. Croix. Before Fountain Valley, St. Croix was on its way to becoming a significant resort destination. Hotels, condominiums, rental villas and private homes were sprouting up all over the landscape.

The boom came to a screeching halt in 1972 after eight people were shot dead at the Fountain Valley Golf Course clubhouse in an armed robbery by five Crucian gunmen. Although a black man was among the victims, the attack was interpreted as racist by many, and constant reiteration of the event keeps alive the perception in many minds that St. Croix is a dangerous place, especially for white people. The fact is that nothing remotely similar happened before or since.

I like to think that all people—West Indian, continental, tourist and space visitor—are as safe here as anywhere, assuming they aren't involved in the drug culture. I don't think it's necessary to be paranoid about personal safety, to live behind bars or in a gated community.

As for going to town at night, anyone basically streetwise is likely to be fine. Those who get into trouble usually have strayed into a tough neighborhood after dark, worn lots of expensive-looking jewelry or appeared obviously under the influence in public. They were natural targets.

Preserving Paradise

One of the reasons many of us pull up stakes and move to a tropical island is the abundance of unspoiled natural beauty here. The air is pure, we are surrounded by clear clean water, and we can live close to nature.

That's the ideal, but not always the reality. Since the emergence of tourism as a cure-all for island economies, many island governments, in their rush to cash in on a boom, have been negligent about protecting those very assets that visitors come to enjoy. Their struggling economies welcome any influx of revenue and jobs, and they allow development that destroys the islands' fragile resources.

St. Croix is still relatively undeveloped and unspoiled in 2001, more by terrible accident than design. One building boom ended abruptly in 1972 after the Fountain Valley shootings. Just as the island was recovering from that tragedy and development was back on the fast track, Hurricane Hugo struck in 1989. By stopping development cold, both disastrous events bought time for the island's environment.

Yet its future is precarious because the territorial government does not yet give the environment the protection it needs. At the end of 2001, despite threats from the federal government and promises from the local government, an old and patched up sewage system often sends untreated waste into the pristine sea, and our solid waste piles up at landfills that violate federal regulations.

Worse, the government has dragged its heels over a land and water use plan to direct development. A plan that finally passed the legislature early in the 1990s is still waiting for a governor's signature at the end of 2001.

Without a law to guide it, the Coastal Zone Management Commission operates in limbo. This is the agency mandated to grant construction permits that balance economic growth with environmental protection but, without a plan that clearly states preservation and conservation requirements, the commissioners understandably have made some uninformed decisions. They are political appointees and rarely have any scientific background.

Thus sediment has been allowed to wash into the sea, smothering coral reefs. Beaches, wetlands and ponds have been altered, breaking the food chain and destroying habitat for fish and wildlife.

In lieu of adequate enforceable government regulations, citizen activists have stepped in and successfully averted several potential environmental catastrophes. The most crucial work has been done by the St. Croix Environmental Association (SEA), a non-profit volunteer organization that has saved ecologically fragile sites from destructive development through persistent advocacy and litigation.

Probably its most important rescue mission was Salt River Bay, which has a complete network of ecosystems, from hilltop through mangrove forest and seagrass beds to coral reef and submarine canyon. It is the only uninterrupted continuum left in the Virgin Islands, maybe the entire Caribbean, and is an important habitat for birds and sea life.

SEA fought the construction of a large resort (hotel/condos/marina) on the bay for six years and finally defeated the proposal, opening the door for the National Park Service to step in and designate the bay and all its surrounding land as a historical park and ecological preserve.

Founded largely by continentals, SEA now reaches deep into the community through a broad educational program, and I like to think the general population will soon be so well-informed it will force the government to provide appropriate guidelines and enforce compliance.

This is my cause. I belong to many worthy community organizations on St. Croix but I concentrate my volunteer work and money on SEA because I believe nothing is more important for the island than protecting its very nature from irreversible harm.

I think of the island's magnificent natural resources as the endowment on which its future depends. As long as it remains an unspoiled natural paradise, the Gentle Virgin will always be a nice place to visit and, for those born here and those who have chosen life in the left lane, a great place to live.

THE END

About the Author

Emy Thomas spent her first thirty-three years following a typical middle-class path, growing up in Connecticut, graduating from prestigious schools in the northeast, and working as a journalist in New York City. Then she discovered the tropics and has embraced the islands and their laid-back lifestyle ever since. For over a dozen years home was a sailboat, when she cruised throughout the Caribbean and Pacific with a typical "yachtie," who made wandering a way of life. They visited scores of island paradises. When it was time to leave the boat and settle down the author chose St. Croix in the U.S. Virgin Islands as her permanent home. She built her dream house on a hillside overlooking the Caribbean Sea and finally found her true calling as an author. Her first book, *Home Is Where the Boat Is,* was published in 1993. *Life in the Left Lane* is her second book.

Printed in the United States
1405700005B/103-255